Peter the Rock
— and —
Jacob the Righteous
in the Gospel according to Matthew

Katherine C. Linforth

Copyright © 2025 Katherine C. Linforth
ISBN: 978-1-923078-65-9

Published by Vivid Publishing
A division of Fontaine Publishing Group
P.O. Box 948, Fremantle
Western Australia 6959
www.vividpublishing.com.au

A catalogue record for this book is available from the National Library of Australia

All rights reserved. No part of this publication may be reproduced, stored in a retrieval system or transmitted in any form or by any means, electronic, mechanical, photocopying, recording or otherwise, without the prior written permission of the copyright holder.

*My deep gratitude to Liam Price,
for his invaluable help and encouragement*

Contents

Chapter One	Introduction	7
Chapter Two	Jacob	13
Chapter Three	Peter	30
Chapter Four	The genealogy. Matthew 1:1-17	41
Chapter Five	The temptations. Matthew 4:1-11	64
Chapter Six	Jesus calls his first four disciples. Matthew 4:18-22	75
Chapter Seven	Anger against a brother. Matthew 5:21-26	78
Chapter Eight	First, Simon. Matthew 10:1-2	90
Chapter Nine	A sparrow falls to the ground. Matthew 10:24-33	93
Chapter Ten	The *mikros* and the *skandalon*. Matthew 18:1-35	103
Chapter Eleven	Between the sanctuary and the altar. Matthew 23:29-37a	115
Chapter Twelve	The redemption and death of Peter. Matthew 14:22-33	120
Epilogue		136
Bibliography		139

– Chapter One –

Introduction

In 62 C.E., in Jerusalem, a man was thrown down from a high point (the 'little wing') of the temple. The fall did not kill him outright: he was stoned, and then his head was beaten in with a launderer's wooden club. The man's killing was a judicial execution, as he had been declared guilty of transgressing the Law in such a manner that the penalty was death by stoning.

The man was Jacob[1] the Righteous - called 'righteous' because he was regarded as exceptionally observant of the Law. To the many who were followers of Jesus the Christ/Messiah, Jacob was also known as "the Lord's brother" (Gal 1:19). That is, Jacob was one of the brothers of Jesus – the first-named of Jesus' four brothers in the Gospels according to Mark (6:3) and Matthew (13:55).[2]

There are three brief, but significant, references to Jacob in the Acts of the Apostles. After Simon Peter, the foremost of Jesus' disciples, left Jerusalem in the early forties, Jacob seems to have become the leader of the Christian Jewish community in Jerusalem (Acts 12:17). Jacob's position of authority is evident some years later, in the

---

1 'James' in English translations.
2 Mt 13:56 also has a reference to Jesus' sisters.

account of the council in Jerusalem, which was convened to discuss the obligations of Gentile Christians in regard to Jewish Law. It is Jacob who gives the decisions regarding the observances required of Gentile Christians in regard to Jewish teaching and practice (Acts 15:13-21). In the late fifties, when Paul makes his final visit to Jerusalem, Jacob is the leader of the elders of the community with whom Paul meets (Acts 21:17-18).

That Jacob's influence extended beyond Jerusalem and Judea is shown in the confrontation between Paul and Peter at Antioch, with the arrival of the "men from James" (Gal 2:11-12). Consequently, Jacob's execution would have profoundly shocked and distressed many, and reverberations would have been felt in all Christian communities (whether Jewish or Gentile) throughout the diaspora.

Not only those who were followers of Jesus were affected by this savage event. According to the Jewish historian Josephus, "those of the inhabitants of the city [Jerusalem] who were considered the most fair-minded and who were strict in observance of the law were offended at this [the execution of Jacob]."[3] These "fair-minded" citizens may well have been Pharisees. Their protests resulted in the deposition of the then high priest, Ananus, son of Annas (himself a former high priest).[4] Ananus's term as high priest was a mere three

---

3   Josephus, *Jewish Antiquities*, Books XVIII-XX, Louis H. Feldman, trans., Loeb Classical Library (London: William Heinemann/Cambridge, Mass.: Harvard University Press, 1965), 495, 497.

4   Brooke Foss Westcott, *The Gospel according to St John* (London: James Clarke, 1958), 254-255: "Annas (or Hanan, Ananias, Ananus) is one of the most remarkable figures in the Jewish history of the time. His unexampled fortune was celebrated in that he himself and his five sons held the high-priesthood in succession. He was high-priest himself from A.D. 7-14 (Jos. 'Ant.' XVIII. 2.l.f.); then, after a short time his son Eleazar held the office for a year; and after a year's interval, his son-in-law Joseph Caiaphas succeeded and held the office till A.D. 35-6 (Jos. *l.c.*). Another son of Annas succeeded Caiaphas, and three other sons afterwards held the office, the last of whom, who bore his father's name, put to death James the brother of the Lord (Jos. 'Ant.' XX.8.1). This mere record reveals the skilful intriguer who exercised through members of his family the headship of his party

months, but that was long enough to bring about the death of Jacob.

In my book, *The Beloved Disciple: Jacob the Brother of the Lord*,[5] I explore the hypothesis that 'the disciple whom Jesus loved,' in John's Gospel, is none other than Jesus' brother Jacob – a boy twelve years of age at the time of Jesus' crucifixion. I believe, through my study of the Greek text of certain passages in John's Gospel, that this hypothesis is validated.

But I discovered more than the fact of young Jacob being Jesus' Beloved Disciple. It became apparent to me that behind the story of the illness, death, and raising to life of 'Lazarus' (Jn 11:1-44) lay the factual account of the execution of the adult Jacob in 62 C.E.. In other words, the Johannine evangelist is the creator of the Lazarus narrative, which he has placed within the story of Jesus' life, shortly before Jesus enters into his Passion, death and resurrection.[6]

According to John's Gospel, it was on account of Lazarus that "many of the Jews were going away and believing in Jesus" (Jn 12:11). In the eyes of the conservative religious-political establishment this would amount to apostasy, and 'Lazarus' would be seen to be leading this apostasy. John's Gospel tells us: "So the chief priests planned to put Lazarus also to death, because on account of him many of the Jews were going away and believing in Jesus" (Jn 12:10-11). Is this why Jacob was killed? Was the Jesus-Messiah movement in Jerusalem still so strong, in 62 C.E., that it was seen as a threat by the religious-political establishment?

Yet why did it take so long after Jesus' death (c30 C.E.) for the

---

(comp. Luke iii.2; Acts iv.6). In the Talmud ... we find a curse on 'the family of Hanan and their serpent-hissings' (comp. Matt. iii.7). The relationship of Caiaphas to Annas is not mentioned by any writer except St John, and yet this relationship alone explains how Caiaphas was able to retain his office by the side of Annas and his sons."

5   Katherine C. Linforth, *The Beloved Disciple: Jacob the Brother of the Lord* (Fremantle, W.A.: VIVID Publishing, 2014).

6   Linforth, *Beloved Disciple*, 111-152.

high-priestly family of Annas (with like-minded others) to take steps to have Jacob the Righteous silenced, on a charge of transgressing the Law? Was there suddenly a new factor which enabled Jacob's opponents to move against him? I believe that the answer to the last question is 'yes'; that something happened which led inevitably to Jacob's death, and I also believe that this involved Peter, Jesus' 'first' disciple.

The history of the present work

In 2008 I undertook a study of the Gospel according to Matthew. It was during the course of that semester that I realised two things: first, how much the Matthean Evangelist was speaking to, and indirectly about, his own Christian community; and second, that the Matthean portrait of Simon Peter was ambivalent, to say the least. (This was before I had discovered Arlo Nau's *Peter in Matthew: Discipleship, Diplomacy, and Dispraise*,[7] and Robert H. Gundry's *Peter: False Disciple and Apostate according to Saint Matthew*.[8])

In 2008 and into the first semester of 2009, I worked on a study of Peter in Matthew's Gospel, of which an edited 12,000-word version (titled "The Judgement of Peter") was submitted as a unit in Biblical Studies. However, I omitted almost all references to Peter's relationship with Jacob – a relationship which, I believe, led eventually to Jacob's death.

On the face of it, such a claim – that Peter (according to Matthew) was ultimately responsible for Jacob's death – may seem preposterous. Matthew's Gospel has only two overt references to Jacob ('James') the brother of Jesus (Mt 13:55; 27:56), and even these

---

7   Arlo J. Nau, *Peter in Matthew: Discipleship, Diplomacy, and Dispraise* (Collegeville, Minnesota: The Liturgical Press, 1992), 24. "The Matthean depiction of Peter is a literary, emotional, and theological rollercoaster for anyone who sensitively reads the First Gospel cover to cover."

8   Robert H. Gundry, *Peter: False Disciple and Apostate according to Saint Matthew* (Grand Rapids, Michigan/Cambridge, U.K.: Williams B. Eerdmans, 2015).

are incidental to the main narrative. Jacob's death occurred more than thirty years after the death of Jesus, and therefore would not be part of Matthew's 'Jesus story.' Yet nearly all biblical scholars identify a Matthean community hovering as a background to the 'Jesus story' – a community which is being addressed through Jesus' teaching; a community which would still hold the memory of the execution of Jesus' brother, Jacob the Righteous.

I have come to believe that Jacob's death (and Peter's part in contributing to that death) has been written as a subtext in Matthew's Gospel. Matthew was a devoutly Jewish Evangelist: he would have been distraught by Jacob's execution and the events connected with it. It is possible – even likely - that Matthew had known Jacob personally.

The Matthean portrait of Peter is distinctive in its treatment. Peter is the 'first' named of the chosen Twelve (Mt 10:2), and is given the distinction of being called by Jesus 'Rock' (*petros*: a variant of the Greek *petra*, meaning 'rock') on which Jesus' church will be built, and against which the gates of hell will not prevail (Mt 16:18). Peter is the only one of Jesus' disciples whose speech is given firsthand – all at moments of great significance (Mt 14:28, 30; 15:15; 16:16, 22; 17:4, 25-26; 18:21; 19:27; 26:33, 35, 69-70, 72, 74). Of the Twelve disciples Peter is the only one whom Jesus addresses by name (Mt 16:17-18).

The Matthean portrait of Peter is one aspect of this Gospel. A second aspect is the palpable sense of anger, and the warnings of judgement that run throughout. There is an unrelenting diatribe (given through the words of Jesus) against those who deserve to be sent to "outer darkness" (8:12; 22:13; 25:30), or cast into the "fire" (3:10, 12; 7:19; 13:40, 42, 50), the "hell of fire" (5:22; 18:9), or the "eternal fire" (18:8; 25:41). Those who suffer this deserved fate will find themselves weeping and gnashing their teeth (8:12; 13:42, 50; 22:13; 24:51; 25:30).

Somewhat at odds with 'judgement,' Matthew's Gospel emphasises the requirement of forgiving a brother who sins against you, no matter how many times that will be called for. Forgiveness of a brother is to be unlimited (Mt 18:21-22). Yet this Evangelist does not seem to have a merciful, forgiving view of the sinners he condemns; rather, he seems to have something/someone very specific in mind.

At whom is all of this anger directed? Was Matthew's community such a desperately sinful lot, unashamedly flouting all the teachings of Jesus? At some point in my study of this Gospel I came to believe that it is Simon Peter who is Matthew's primary target, with the warnings of "outer darkness," "hell of fire," and "weeping and gnashing of teeth." Why would this be? Surely Peter's denials of Jesus (in a Gospel written perhaps forty years after Jesus' death) would not be enough to earn him a (Matthean) fate reserved for the wicked and demonic? After all, Peter was the only one of the Twelve brave enough to follow Jesus to the high priest's courtyard, when Jesus was arrested (Mt 26:58; Mk 14:54; Lk 22:54-55; Jn 18:15-16). So was there something else about Simon Peter – something not in the 'Jesus story' – which Matthew found (almost) unforgivable? I say 'almost,' because I believe that Matthew has, in his Gospel, a redemptive episode concerning Simon Peter.

It would be more than helpful for readers of this present work to be acquainted with the hypothesis worked through in *The Beloved Disciple: Jacob the Brother of the Lord*. Before looking at Matthew's Gospel we need to take a closer look at the two protagonists – Simon Peter and Jacob – to gain some understanding of their temperaments, their abilities, and their commitment to Jesus and his mission.

All New Testament Biblical quotations are from the R.S.V. Interlinear Greek-English New Testament,[9] unless otherwise stated. Quotations from Hebrew scripture are from the New Revised Standard Version.

---

[9] *The R.S.V. Interlinear Greek-English New Testament. The Nestle Greek Text with a Literal English Translation*, 3rd ed., Alfred Marshall, ed. (London: Samuel Bagster, 1975).

Chapter Two

Jacob

What were they like, these two men; Simon Peter and Jacob? What do we know of their backgrounds, their upbringings, their personalities, their roles in the Jesus-Messiah movement? Let us start with the younger one - Jesus' brother Jacob. His name is Jacob (Gk: *Iakōbos*), but it has been translated into English as 'James.' This unfortunate translation negates his heritage; the fact that this Jacob was named after one of the great Hebrew patriarchs – Jacob, the son of Isaac, the son of Abraham.[10]

The Gospels of Mark and Matthew put Jacob's name first in the list of the four brothers of Jesus (Mk 6:3: "James [Jacob] and Joses and Judas and Simon"; Mt 13:55: "James [Jacob] and Joseph and Simon and Judas"). As the first-listed of the brothers, do we conclude that Jacob was the eldest, or was Jacob named first by these Gospel writers

---

10 John Painter, *Just James: The Brother of Jesus in History and Tradition* (Columbia, South Carolina: University of South Carolina Press, 1997), 3. "The differentiated use of the two forms of the name in the New Testament, where figures in 'Christian' history are given the hellenized form while those from Jewish history prior to Jesus, especially the patriarch Jacob, retain the Semitic form, may have led the English translators of the Bible to retain *Jacob* as an Old Testament name, while using *James* as the name for the Christian apostles. The two names in English are derived from Latin, in which *Jacobus* and *Jacomus* are variants of the same name."

because he became so eminent within the Jerusalem Jesus-Messiah community? I believe it was the latter – that in fact, while Jacob may have been one of the younger brothers of Jesus, Jacob was the one closest in temperament to Jesus, the one who understood Jesus more than did the other brothers, and who became in effect the 'heir-apparent' when Jesus was facing arrest and execution.

Presumably Jacob, as a son of Mary and Joseph, was brought up in the small town of Nazareth, in Galilee.[11] According to Matthew 13:55 and Mark 6:3, Joseph was a *tektōn*, which could mean that he was a carpenter, or possibly a builder.[12] It seems that Joseph may not have lived long enough to see his children grow up, in which case Jesus, as the eldest of the children of Mary and Joseph, would have had a responsible role as eldest male of the family – becoming almost a father-figure to Jacob and his siblings. This, of course, is supposition, but not unreasonable supposition.

Mikros: Jacob's nickname

In *The Beloved Disciple: Jacob the Brother of the Lord*, I put forward the hypothesis that Jacob was a boy of twelve when his brother Jesus was crucified.[13] In connection with this youthfulness of Jacob is the other conclusion I came to, that he was given the nickname *Mikros* as a child, and was known, or referred to, by this nickname even in adulthood. This was the key which unlocked for me the story of Jacob – the 'disciple whom Jesus loved' (amongst other pseudonyms), of John's Gospel.

---

11 Mk 1:9; Mt 2:23; Lk 2:4; Jn 1:45.

12 W.D. Davies and Dale C. Allison, *A Critical and Exegetical Commentary on The Gospel According to Saint Matthew*, Vol. 2, Matthew VIII-XVIII (London/New York: T&T Clark, 2004), 456. "The Greek word, τεκτων, most commonly means 'mason', 'carpenter', 'woodworker'. Other attested meanings include 'artisan', 'contractor', 'builder' ... "

13 Katherine C. Linforth, *The Beloved Disciple: Jacob the Brother of the Lord* (Fremantle, W.A.: VIVID Publishing, 2014), 24-26.

In the New Testament, only once does the word *mikros* occur in connection with the name 'Jacob' (*Iakōbos*), and that is in Mark's description of the bystanders at Jesus' crucifixion (Mk 15:40).

There were also women looking on from afar, among whom were Mary Magdalene, and Mary the mother of James [Jacob] the younger (*Iakōbou tou mikrou*) ... "[14]

Iakōbou tou mikrou can mean either 'Jacob the young [one]' or 'Jacob the small [one].' Was he, in fact, the youngest of Mary's and Joseph's sons, and therefore 'small'? Was he perhaps physically small all his life? I believe *Mikros* was the nickname given to young Jacob by his siblings and friends, and would have been remembered and used by them even when Jacob became an adult.

(A nickname seemed to be a common feature within the inner group of Jesus' disciples. Simon is renamed Cephas/Peter, meaning 'Rock'[15]; and James and John of Zebedee are called 'Boanerges,' meaning 'sons of thunder,'[16] according to Mark 3:17.)

The few references to Jacob in the New Testament tell us almost nothing about him, yet the adult Jacob was a figure of enormous significance and influence, within Jerusalem and also for the Christian Jewish communities of the diaspora. In the Gospels of Mark and Matthew we know of him by name only as a boy. As already mentioned, Jacob is the first-named of Jesus' four brothers (Mk 6:3; Mt 13:55). Jacob's name is associated with his mother Mary, at the crucifixion (Mk 15:40; Mt 27:56), and with the Mary who goes to Jesus' tomb (Mk 16:1; Lk 24:10).

Jacob is never named in John's Gospel, yet his story is the ongoing 'hidden' story that John tells, behind the story of the life, death and

---

14 Linforth, *Beloved Disciple*, 23-29.
15 Mk 3:16; Mt 16:18; Lk 6:14; Jn 1:42.
16 See Linforth, *Beloved Disciple*, 202, Footnote 386.

resurrection of Jesus. He is the anonymous disciple of John 1:35-40[17]; the young boy who shares his bread and fish (Jn 6:8-9)[18]; 'Lazarus' (Jn 11:1-48)[19]; "the disciple whom Jesus loved" (Jn 13:23; 19:26; 20:2; 21:7, 20)[20]; the coming Paraclete/Spirit of Truth (Jn 14:16-17, 25-26; 15:26; 16:7, 13)[21]; and he is the "another/other" unnamed disciple who goes with Jesus into the courtyard of the high priest (Jn 18:15-16).[22]

It is only in the Acts of the Apostles, Paul's first letter to the Corinthians, and Paul's letter to the Galatians that we hear of the adult Jacob. The author of Acts mentions Jacob three times (Acts 12:17; 15:13; 21:18), but omits any explanation as to who he is (such as, 'the brother of the Lord') or of his importance in the Christian Jewish Christian community in Jerusalem.

Jacob in the Acts of the Apostles

Acts 12:17

The first mention of Jacob in Acts is after Simon Peter has miraculously escaped from prison, and has to leave Jerusalem. Before Peter does so, he returns to the house of Mary (John Mark's mother; Acts 12:12) and tells the believers gathered there about his escape and his imminent departure from Jerusalem. Peter says, "Tell this to James [Jacob] and to the brethren" (Acts 12:17). It is assumed that the readers of Acts know who this James (Jacob) is. Obviously he is not James of Zebedee, who has been beheaded by order of Herod Agrippa I (Acts 12:1-2), yet the writer of Acts gives no information which would identify this James (Jacob).

---

17 Linforth, *Beloved Disciple*, 93-99.
18 Linforth, *Beloved Disciple*, 100-105.
19 Linforth, *Beloved Disciple*, 111-152.
20 Linforth, *Beloved Disciple*, 153-161.
21 Linforth, *Beloved Disciple*, 162-179.
22 Linforth, *Beloved Disciple*, 181-191.

I take this incident to imply that Jacob was a highly significant figure in the Jesus-Messiah movement, and that, with Simon Peter's departure from Jerusalem, Jacob became leader in his own right. How old would he have been? I have suggested an age of about twenty-six, if these events occurred in about 44 C.E.[23] Jacob is not only the brother of Jesus, but he has attained the maturity to guide the young Jesus-Messiah community in Jerusalem, as well as the scattered Christian Jewish communities of the diaspora.

In these years since the crucifixion of Jesus, has Simon Peter been a mentor/father-figure to Jacob, preparing him for the time when he (Jacob) would take on the role of leader of the community? There are hints of this possibility, in Paul's letter to the Galatians (Gal 1:18-19), which we will look at further on.[24]

Acts 15:13-21

In the narrative concerning the Council of Jerusalem the writer of Acts is again not forthcoming about the identity of Jacob, nor his significance within the Jesus-Messiah communities of Jerusalem and elsewhere.[25] Peter, Paul and Barnabas are all present, and Peter gives an impassioned speech regarding the eligibility of Gentile believers to be acknowledged by the Jewish believers:

> And God who knows the heart bore witness to them, giving them the Holy Spirit just as he did to us; and he made no distinction between us and them, but cleansed their hearts by faith. Now therefore why do you make trial of God by

---

[23] Linforth, *Beloved Disciple*, 40-41.

[24] John 20:3-10 also hints at this relationship between Peter and Jacob ('the disciple whom Jesus loved'). See Linforth, *Beloved Disciple*, 199-202.

[25] The Council of Jerusalem is dated approx. 48-51 C.E.. L.C.A. Alexander, "Chronology of Paul," in *Dictionary of Paul and his Letters*, Gerald F. Hawthorne, Ralph P. Martin, Daniel G. Reid, eds. (Downers Grove, Illinois/ Leicester, England: InterVarsity Press, 1993), 122-123. This would put Jacob at the age of thirty, or early thirties.

putting a yoke upon the neck of the disciples which neither
our fathers nor we have been able to bear? (Acts 15:8-10).

Peter's speech is very interesting, in regard to the stance of both Peter and Jacob to the inclusion of Gentile believers. Here Peter seems almost to disregard any value in making the Gentile believers observe all or parts of the Mosaic Law ('a yoke'). Yet it is not Peter but Jacob who pronounces regarding the basic practices to be required of Gentile followers of Jesus.

Therefore my judgment is that we should not trouble those
of the Gentiles who turn to God, but should write to them
to abstain from the pollutions of idols and from unchastity
and from what is strangled and from blood (Acts 15:19-20).

Paul and Barnabas return to Antioch, in company with others from Jerusalem, to deliver a letter to the believers there, informing them of what the Council had agreed upon. The circumcision of male believers – surely one of the most confronting possibilities – would not be required. However, the issue of communal meals for Jewish and Gentile believers had not been addressed, and this would become a flash-point between Peter and Paul (and, indirectly, Jacob).

In this account of the Council, Jacob's name is mentioned only once (Acts 15:13), yet he is obviously the person with the greatest authority. For the rest of the narrative, Jacob is subsumed in the catch-all phrase "the apostles and the elders" (Acts 15:4, 6, 22).

Acts 21:17-18
Several years after the Council, the writer of Acts gives Jacob a final mention, when Paul returns to Jerusalem before going on to Rome.[26] "When we had come to Jerusalem, the brethren received us gladly. On the following day Paul went in with us to James {Jacob}; and all

---

26 This was Paul's last visit to Jerusalem, and it would be the last time he met with Jacob. The voyage to Rome would only take place after Paul had been two years in custody at Caesarea Maritima.

the elders were present" (Acts 21:17-18). It seems to be assumed that Jacob had a leading role among the elders, but nothing is said about it. If Paul was in Jerusalem in about 57-59 C.E.,[27] then I believe Jacob would be in his late thirties or early forties.

Jacob (and Peter/Cephas) in the letters of Paul
1 Corinthians 15:3-8

We turn now to Paul's letters, and their references to Jacob, the brother of Jesus. Jacob is mentioned in Paul's first letter to the church at Corinth (dated some time between 52 and 57 C.E.[28]). We learn that Paul had been told (years prior to this letter) that the risen Jesus appeared to Jacob, after Jesus' death and resurrection, although Peter ('Cephas' as Paul refers to him) is credited with being the first person to whom the risen Jesus appeared.

> For I delivered to you as of first importance what I also received, that Christ died for our sins in accordance with the scriptures, that he was buried, that he was raised on the third day in accordance with the scriptures, and that he appeared to Cephas [Peter], then to the twelve. Then he appeared to more than five hundred brethren at one time, most of whom are still alive, though some have fallen asleep. Then he appeared to James [Jacob],[29] then to all the

---

27 Alexander, "Chronology," 122-123.

28 Alexander, "Chronology," 122-123.

29 There is an account of an appearance by the risen Jesus to his brother Jacob, in The Gospel of the Hebrews, recorded by Jerome in *De viris inlustribus* 2, in *The Other Bible*, Willis Barnstone, ed. (New York: HarperCollins, 2005), 335. "And when the Lord had given the linen cloth to the servant of the priest, he went to James [Jacob] and appeared to him. For James [Jacob] had sworn that he would not eat bread from that hour in which had had drunk the cup of the Lord until he should see him risen from among them that sleep. And shortly thereafter the Lord said: Bring a table and bread! And immediately it is added: he took the bread, blessed it and brake it and gave it to James [Jacob] the Just and said to him: My brother, eat your bread, for the Son of man is risen from among them that sleep."

apostles. Last of all, as to one untimely born, he appeared also to me. (1 Cor 15:3-8)

When did Paul 'receive' this information about appearances of the risen Lord? Surely it was when he first visited Peter in Jerusalem, and at the same time met with the young Jacob (Gal 1:18-19). Paul's own encounter with the risen Lord must have been the foundation of his talks with the other two, and, likewise, they must have recounted their own experiences to Paul.

Paul credits both Peter and Jacob as having had an appearance to them of the risen Lord, with Peter's being the first; yet the Gospels do not say this about Peter. The only Gospel reference which could imply this is Luke 24:33-35, which almost seems like an interpolation in the story of the two people who met the risen Jesus on the road to Emmaus.

Galatians 1:18-19
In his letter to the Galatian Christian community Paul refers three times to Jacob, each time in a different context. In the first reference Paul is looking back to his trip to Jerusalem, when he went to visit Peter (Cephas), some time after his (Paul's) life-changing experience on his way to Damascus.

> Then after three years I went up to Jerusalem to visit Cephas [Peter], and remained with him fifteen days. But I saw none of the other apostles except James [Jacob] the Lord's brother. (Gal 1:18-19).

Paul is writing, in about 54 C.E.,[30] of his meeting with Cephas and Jacob at some time in the early-to mid-thirties, when I estimate Jacob to have been about fifteen or sixteen years of age. Biblical scholars discuss whether Paul includes Jacob in the term 'apostles,' because

---

30 Joseph A. Fitzmyer, "*The Letter to the Galatians*," in *The New Jerome Biblical Commentary*, Raymond E. Brown, Joseph A. Fitzmyer, Roland E. Murphy, eds. (London: Geoffrey Chapman, 1993), 781.

there is ambiguity in the way Paul phrases it. With our knowledge of the youthfulness of Jacob at this time, Paul could not have meant that Jacob was (also) an apostle, and yet Jacob's significance, as 'heir-apparent' to Jesus in the Jesus-Messiah movement, could not be passed over. One could hardly describe Jacob, at this stage, as an 'apostle,' and yet his future importance for the Christian communities would be undeniable.

This brief account of the meeting of Paul with Peter/Cephas and Jacob, at Jerusalem, conjures up many questions and much speculation. For Paul, Peter was the leading person of the Jesus-Messiah movement - the person with whom Paul wanted to talk about his (Paul's) experience of meeting the risen Jesus, and of Jesus' ministry, death, and resurrection. Paul is definite that he saw none of the other apostles at this time, yet he mentions meeting Jacob, the Lord's brother. Nothing further is said about Jacob, and it is apparent that, for Paul, Peter is the most important figure.

What about the adolescent Jacob? Could he hold his own with Paul, in conversation and discussion? Jacob came from a modest village environment in Galilee. But if, after Jesus' crucifixion, Jacob stayed on in Jerusalem, then more than likely he was receiving an education, or at least a training, which his natural intelligence and memory took on board.[31] Most importantly, he was Jesus' brother, and both he and Peter had known Jesus in the flesh, had heard Jesus teach, had seen him do acts of healing and power, and had seen the risen Jesus after his crucifixion (1 Cor 15:3-8).

Galatians 2:1-2

In the same letter Paul recounts another, more recent meeting with Jacob, Peter/Cephas and John, in Jerusalem.

Then after fourteen years I went up again to Jerusalem with

---

31 Linforth, *Beloved Disciple*, 183.

Barnabas, taking Titus along with me. I went up by revelation; and I laid before them (but privately before those who were of repute) the gospel which I preach among the Gentiles, lest somehow I should be running or had run in vain. (Gal 2:1-2)

Those who were "of repute" included Jacob, Peter (Cephas), and John. Giving this meeting a tentative date of between 48 and 51 C.E.,[32] Jacob would have been in his early thirties. For the purposes of this study of Jacob and Peter, it is important to note the outcome of the discussion: "when they perceived the grace that was given to me, James [Jacob] and Cephas [Peter] and John, who were reputed to be pillars, gave to me and Barnabas the right hand of fellowship, that we should go to the Gentiles and they to the circumcised ..." (Gal 2:9). Paul seems quite certain that his own mission was to the Gentiles, and Peter's mission was to other Jews –"the circumcised."

Jacob is the first-named of the "pillars" – signifying his role of authority and leadership. The result of the meeting seems straightforward. Paul is given encouragement and authority to make his mission the conversion of the Gentiles, while Peter's mission is to fellow-Jews.

However, Paul wastes no time in his letter to the Galatian church in speaking of Peter's (Cephas's) 'insincerity,' when Cephas comes to the Antioch community. The incident indirectly involves Jacob - but to what degree is debatable.

Gal 2:11-12

> But when Cephas [Peter] came to Antioch I opposed him to his face, because he stood condemned. For before certain men came from James [Jacob], he ate with the Gentiles; but when they came he drew back and separated himself, fearing the circumcision party. (Gal 2:11-12)

---

32 Alexander, "Chronology," 122-123.

Who were these "certain men" from Jacob? Were they sent expressly by Jacob, to search out any irregularities that might be occurring in a mixed (i.e. Gentile and Jewish) Christian community? Or were these men on another errand, but became focussed on what was to them (as members of the 'circumcision party') a serious breach of the Mosaic Law?[33]

Apparently Peter had been happy to share meals with the Gentile believers, although his mission was strictly to 'the 'circumcised.' With the arrival of the Jews from Jerusalem, he and other Jewish believers stopped having meals with the Gentile believers. We simply don't know how tightly Jacob held to the Law, in regard to Jesus-Messiah communities where there was a mixture of Jews and Gentiles. Likewise, we don't know how strongly Peter held to the requirements of the Law, but one gathers that he was flexible, in circumstances which seemed to him to require flexibility.

Jacob took on the role of authority figure in the early forties, while Peter was moving out into the much wider, cosmopolitan world which included Syrian Antioch, probably Corinth, and Rome. In his contact with such cultures Peter may well have developed a more relaxed attitude to Jewish Law, and moved further towards the position of Paul in regard to Gentile believers.

---

33 Donald Guthrie, *Galatians* (Grand Rapids, Michigan: Wm B. Eerdmans/London: Marshall, Morgan & Scott, 1981), 84. "**certain men came from James [Jacob]:** this expression may be compared with Ac. 15.1, where there is a reference to some men coming down from Judea. There can be no question that these belonged to the circumcision party, which believed that all Gentiles should be circumcised, and which was apparently appealing to the authority of James [Jacob] in support of their demands. If they had been commissioned by James [Jacob] personally, it would be extremely difficult to harmonise this with James' [Jacob's] action reported in verse 9, unless some considerable interval separated the events. Since this is unlikely it is more probable that these men were doing some special mission under the direction of James [Jacob] and had not been specifically sent to spy out the position regarding Jewish-Gentile fellowship. They possibly protested when they saw what had happened and their protests may have been the occasion of Peter's inconsistency, since he wished to avoid a rift."

In closing, we note that Peter had enough 'clout' apparently, that all the other Christian Jews at Antioch (including Barnabas, who had initially brought Paul into the Christian community; Acts 9:26-27) followed Peter's lead in separating from the Gentile believers when it came to meals.

Jacob in non-canonical literature

In contrast to the paucity of information about Jacob in the New Testament, there is a considerable body of non-canonical literature which speaks of Jacob, Jesus' brother. Eusebius, the fourth-century bishop and church historian, quotes from Clement:

> Peter and James and John after the Ascension of the Saviour did not struggle for glory, because they had previously been given honour by the Saviour, but chose James the Just (*Iakōbon ton dikaion*) as bishop of Jerusalem.[34]

It is my belief that Clement (and therefore Eusebius) are mistaken in saying that James the Just took on leadership as "bishop" straight after Jesus' Ascension. I believe Jacob was a boy of twelve at the time of his brother's crucifixion, and only took on leadership of the Jesus-Messiah community when Peter was forced to leave Jerusalem in the early forties.[35]

Clement says further:

> After the Resurrection the Lord gave the tradition of knowledge to James the Just and John and Peter, these gave it to the other Apostles and the other Apostles to the seventy, of whom Barnabas also was one. Now there were two Jameses, one James the Just, who was thrown down from the pinnacle of the temple and beaten to death with a

---

[34] Eusebius, *The Ecclesiastical History*, Books I-IV, Kirsopp Lake, trans., Loeb Classical Library (Cambridge, Mass.: London: Harvard University Press, 1926), 105.

[35] Linforth, *Beloved Disciple*, 40-42.

fuller's club, and the other he who was beheaded.³⁶

Eusebius gives us a description of the adult Jacob, this time quoting Hegesippus, "who belongs to the generation after the Apostles"³⁷:

> The charge of the Church passed to James [Jacob] the brother of the Lord, together with the Apostles. He was called the 'Just (*dikaios*)' by all men from the Lord's time to ours, since many are called James [Jacob], but he was holy from his mother's womb. He drank no wine or strong drink, nor did he eat flesh; no razor went upon his head; he did not anoint himself with oil, and he did not go to the baths. He alone was allowed to enter into the sanctuary, for he did not wear wool but linen, and he used to enter alone into the temple and be found kneeling and praying for forgiveness for the people, so that his knees grew hard like a camel's because of his constant worship of God, kneeling and asking forgiveness for the people. So from his excessive righteousness he was called the Just (*dikaios*) and Oblias, that is in Greek, 'Rampart of the people and righteousness (*dikaiosunē*),' as the prophets of the people declare concerning him.³⁸

Hegesippus is describing a man who dedicated himself from his youth to serving his God, in an ascetic lifestyle and with deep piety.

There is no evidence, either way, that Jacob was married or stayed single. Writing to the Corinthians, Paul asks: "Do we not have the right to be accompanied by a sister wife, as the other apostles and the brothers of the Lord and Cephas?"(1 Cor 9:5). It seems unlikely (and I have not found any evidence) that Jacob travelled outside Jerusalem, with or without a wife.

---

36 Eusebius, *Ecclesiastical History* (2.1), 105.
37 Eusebius, *Ecclesiastical History* (2.23), 171.
38 Eusebius, *Ecclesiastical History* (2.23), 171.

Jacob's death

The following account of Jacob's death comes from Eusebius, again quoting Hegesippus. The scribes and Pharisees insist that Jacob stand on the little wing of the temple, and persuade the crowd below "not to err concerning Jesus." Instead, to their fury, he testifies to Jesus as the "Son of Man," sitting in heaven at the right hand of the "great power," and "he will come on the clouds of heaven."[39] Many in the crowd cry out, "Hosanna to the Son of David."[40]

> So they went up and threw down the Just, and they said to one another, 'Let us stone James the Just,' and they began to stone him since the fall had not killed him, but he turned and knelt saying, 'I beseech thee, O Lord, God and Father, forgive them, for they know not what they do.' And while they were thus stoning him one of the priests of the sons of Rechab, the son of Rechabim, to whom Jeremiah the prophet bore witness, cried out saying, 'Stop! What are you doing? The Just is praying for you.' And a certain man among them, one of the laundrymen, took the club with which he used to beat out the clothes, and hit the Just on the head, and so he suffered martyrdom.[41]

The first-century Jewish historian, Josephus, also has an account of Jacob's end – an account which targets the then high priest, Ananus,[42] as being responsible for Jacob's death.

---

39 Eusebius, *Ecclesiastical History* (2.23), 173.

40 Eusebius, *Ecclesiastical History* (2.23), 173, 175.

41 Eusebius, *Ecclesiastical History* (2.23), 175.

42 Raymond E. Brown, *The Death of the Messiah*, Vol. I (New York: Doubleday, 1994), 408. "In AD 6 P. Sulpicius Quirinius, legate in Syria, appointed Annas (Greek: Ananos; Hebrew: *Hananya*) high priest. In 15 Valerius Gratus, prefect in Judea, deposed Annas. He remained a powerful force, however, for in the fifty years after his deposition five of his sons became high priests ... as well as a son-in-law and a grandson." Brown, *Death*, 409. "As far as Christians are concerned, is it accidental that Jesus, Stephen (the first martyr) and James [Jacob] the brother of the Lord were all put to

He [Ananus] followed the school of the Sadducees, who are indeed more heartless than any of the other Jews, as I have already explained, when they sit in judgement. Possessed of such a character, Ananus thought that he had a favourable opportunity because Festus was dead and Albinus was still on the way.[43] And so he convened the judges of the Sanhedrin and brought before them a man named James [Jacob], the brother of Jesus who was called the Christ, and certain others. He accused them of having transgressed the law and delivered them up to be stoned.[44]

Conclusion

How to sum up what we know about Jacob? I believe Jacob was much younger than Peter, perhaps by eighteen or more years. Jacob was nicknamed *Mikros* ('little one') when he was young, and the name stuck: anyone in the Jerusalem Christian community would know that the name *Mikros* meant Jacob the Righteous. Peter probably had a great deal to do with Jacob, following Jesus' death, when Peter took on the leadership of the Christian Jewish community. He would have been a friend, a mentor, perhaps a sort of father-figure to the young boy. Jacob, as Jesus' brother and close companion, would have been seen as the future leader-in the-making.

---

death during the tenure of priests of the house of Annas? Indeed, since Matthias, son of Annas, was high priest in 42/43 under Herod Agrippa ...., possibly James the brother of John (the first of the Twelve to be martyred) also perished under the house of Annas (Acts 12:1-3). That would mean that every famous Christian who died violently in Judea before the Jewish Revolt [66-70 C.E.] suffered in the tenure of a priest related to Annas."

43 Painter, *Just James*, 135. "The death of James [Jacob] took place in a break of Roman administration. When the Roman procurator Festus died, Caesar (Nero) sent Albinus, who, because he had to travel to Judaea via Alexandria, took some time to arrive, probably three or four months."

44 Josephus, *Jewish Antiquities*, Books XVIII-XX, Louis H. Feldman, trans., Loeb Classical Library (London: William Heinemann/Cambridge, Mass.: Harvard University Press, 1965), 495, 497.

The adult Jacob obviously had authority: the incidents recorded in Acts – both at the Council of Jerusalem, and during Paul's last visit to Jerusalem – reveal that Jacob was unmistakably the leading figure of the Christian Jewish community. Paul's letter to the Galatians reveals the authority Jacob had, when even Peter and Barnabas stopped eating with the Gentile believers in Antioch, because of the arrival of the "men from James [Jacob]."

Jacob was strictly obedient to the Mosaic Law, and became known in his lifetime as Jacob the Righteous. Hegesippus's account of Jacob's piety and ascetic lifestyle reveals a man totally dedicated to serving God, and praying for forgiveness for his people.

Jacob's death (unlike that of Jesus) was actually carried out by the Jerusalem hierarchy, led by the high-priestly family of Annas. Both Jacob and Jesus died in Jerusalem, at Passover; Jesus died outside the walls of the city, and Jacob died within the precincts of the temple that was so much a part of his life of prayer.

Matthew's code-words for Jacob

I believe that Matthew, in his Gospel, uses code-words for the two figures (Peter and Jacob) who are the protagonists of a story 'hidden' behind the story of Jesus' birth, ministry, death and resurrection. It is these code-words, creating links between certain episodes of the Gospel, which gradually disclose the circumstances leading up to Jacob's death.

Jacob as an adult, and leader of the Christian Jewish community from the early forties to 62 C.E., was known as 'Jacob the Righteous/Just.' The Greek for 'just/righteous' is: **dikaios**: "conforming to the laws [towards gods and men]"; "just, honest, civil, courteous, hospitable."[45]

The Hebrew equivalent of the Greek *dikaios* is *zadik*, from which

---

45 Franco Montanari, *The Brill Dictionary of Ancient Greek* (Leiden/Boston: Brill, 2015), 529.

comes the personal name of **Zadok**.

I believe that Jacob, from his childhood, was given the nickname[46] *mikros*: "small in size," "small in compass," "small in significance," short in time (or 'young' in age)."[47]

We keep these code-words in mind as we work through Matthew's Gospel.

---

46 See Katherine C. Linforth, *The Beloved Disciple: Jacob the Brother of the Lord* (Fremantle, W.A.: VIVID Publishing, 2014), 26-7.

47 "Mikros," in *Theological Dictionary of the New Testament*, Gerhard Kittel and Gerhard Friedrich, eds., abridged in one volume by Geoffrey W. Bromiley (Grand Rapids, Michigan: William B. Eerdmans, 1985), 593-4.

Chapter Three

Peter

If we had to conjure up a figure who was the antithesis of Jacob – in age, occupation, temperament, and piety – then Simon Peter would surely be considered. Yet the two were so closely linked, from the time that Simon Peter became one of Jesus' disciples (when Jacob was a young boy) to the time of Jacob's death.

What they did have in common was their home territory of Galilee. Although Peter came from Bethsaida,[48] at some point he became a resident of Capernaum, on the north-west coast of the Sea of Galilee. Simon Peter and his brother Andrew were fishermen, and Simon was in partnership with James and John of Zebedee,[49] which means that John of Zebedee (whom I believe to be the author of the Gospel according to John) knew Simon Peter long before they all became Jesus' disciples. Three of them – Simon Peter, and James and John of Zebedee - would become the inner group of Jesus' Twelve chosen disciples, and in the Synoptic Gospels all three are present (and named) at significant moments in the life and ministry of Jesus;

---

48 Jn 1:44. "Now Philip was from Bethsaida, the city of Andrew and Peter."
49 Lk 5:10.

the healing of Peter's mother-in-law,[50] the transfiguration of Jesus on the mountain,[51] and Jesus' time of prayer in Gethsemane.[52]

From references to Peter's mother-in-law (Mk 1:30; Mt 8:14; Lk 4:38) we know that Peter was married. Paul refers to this in writing to the Corinthian church: "Do we not have the right to be accompanied by a sister wife (*adelphēn gunaika*), as the other apostles and the brothers of the Lord and Cephas [Peter]?" (1 Cor 9:5).[53]

Simon Peter, in the Synoptic Gospels, is the first to be called by Jesus to become his disciple,[54] and is the first-named in the list of the chosen Twelve.[55] In fact, Matthew makes Simon Peter's pre-eminence clear in calling Peter 'first': "The names of the twelve apostles are these: first (*prōtos*), Simon, who is called Peter (*Petros*) ... " (Mt 10:2). The significance of this word 'first' will become apparent when we look more closely at Matthew's Gospel.

I am assuming, rather tentatively, that Simon Peter did not have much schooling.[56] There is an occasion in Acts when Peter and John are described by the leading people and rulers of Jerusalem as "uneducated, common men (*anthrōpoi agrammatoi ... kai idiōtai*)" (Acts 4:13). According to Luke Timothy Johnson:

---

50 Mk 1:29-31 (cf. Mt 8:14-15;Lk 4:38-39).
51 Mk 9:2-8; Mt 17:1-8; Lk 9:28-36.
52 Mk 14:32-33; Mt 26:36-37.
53 Non-canonical texts also speak of Peter having a wife and a daughter. Eusebius, *The Ecclesiastical History*, Books I-IV, Kirsopp Lake, trans., Loeb Classical Library (Cambridge, Mass./London: Harvard University Press, 1926), 269. Eusebius quotes Clement: "They say that the blessed Peter when he saw his own wife led out to death rejoiced at her calling and at her return home, and called out to her in true warning and comfort, addressing her by her name, 'Remember the Lord.'" Unfortunately her name was not recorded.
54 Mk 1:16-17; Mt 4:18-19; Lk 5:1-11.
55 Mk 3:14-16; Mt 10:2; Lk 6:13. There is no listing of the Twelve in John's Gospel.
56 And yet John of Zebedee, from a similar fishing background, wrote the work of genius which is the Gospel according to John.

The term *agrammatos* literally means to be illiterate (= without letters), but is extended to mean lack of education generally ... This is the only use in the NT. The term *idiotēs* derives from *idios* and has the first sense of being a 'private person,' and by extension, one who is uncouth and ignorant ... [57]

In the Synoptic Gospels (as in Acts), Peter stands pre-eminent as the spokesman for all the Twelve. (At times he may be speaking solely for himself, as we shall explore in the Gospel of Matthew.) He is the one who asks questions, or answers questions, or responds to situations. In all four Gospels there are important occasions on which Simon Peter speaks (i.e. where his direct speech is given):

1. When Jesus ask his disciples who they think he is, Peter replies, "you are the Christ [that is, the Messiah, the anointed one]."[58]
2. When Peter and James and John of Zebedee see Jesus transfigured, and Elijah and Moses with him, Peter speaks up and suggests erecting three 'booths' (*skēnas*) to honour the three.[59]
3. In the face of imminent danger, Peter pledges unwavering loyalty to Jesus, even to the point of dying with Jesus.[60]
4. From all four Gospels we know that when Jesus is arrested and brought before the high priest, Peter follows Jesus into the high priest's courtyard, where he denies knowing Jesus,

---

57 Luke Timothy Johnson, *The Acts of the Apostles* (Collegeville, Minnesota: The Liturgical Press, 1992), 78.
58 Mk 8:29; Mt 16:15-16; Lk 9:20. In John's Gospel the location and context are quite different, as is Peter's response: "Lord, to whom shall we go? You have the words of eternal life; and we have believed, and have come to know, that you are the Holy One of God" (Jn 6:66-69).
59 Mk 9:5; Mt 17:4; Lk 9:33.
60 Mk 14:27-31; Mt 26:31-35; Lk 22: 31-33: Jn 13:36-37.

or being his disciple.[61]

It is shows the significance of Simon Peter that he is the only individual disciple for whom Jesus prays (Lk 22:31-32).

Peter in Acts

The picture of Peter in the four Gospels is that of an eager follower of Jesus, yet a follower who at times doubts, misunderstands, becomes frightened, and denies Jesus. However, the book of Acts shows Peter as almost a super-figure – a bold, articulate, learned public speaker; a miracle-worker; the authority figure who can reprimand members of the community; a missionary; the one who is led by the Holy Spirit, by means of a vision, to show the 'circumcised' members of the Jesus-followers that Gentiles may be recipients of the same Holy Spirit, and therefore able to become acknowledged Jesus-Messiah followers.

Peter the witness to Jesus' resurrection

According to the Acts of the Apostles, Peter takes on the role of leader of the Jesus-Messiah community in Jerusalem, after Jesus' crucifixion. On the day of Pentecost, Peter speaks to the crowds who have come to Jerusalem for the Passover festival. When the crowds accuse the disciples of being drunk, Peter replies that they are not drunk (at 9 a.m.) but are filled with the Spirit (Acts 2:5-18). Following on a long, bold and confronting speech by Peter(a speech which includes quotes from the prophet Joel and from certain psalms) many people come to repentance, and some three thousand persons are baptized (Acts 2:37-41).

Peter has told the crowd about Jesus' resurrection. "This Jesus God raised up, and of that we are all witnesses" (Acts 2:32). In other words, Peter himself is a witness to the risen Jesus.

---

61 Mk 14:66-71; Mt 26: 69-74; Lk 22:54-60; Jn 18:15-17, 25-27.

Peter the miracle-worker

Peter is able to perform miracles of healing: he heals a lame man (Acts 3:1-10), and testifies to the rulers, elders and scribes that "by the name of Jesus Christ of Nazareth, whom you crucified, whom God raised from the dead, by him this man is standing before you well" (Acts 4:10). The members of the hierarchy admit to each other that this miraculous sign is "manifest to all the inhabitants of Jerusalem, and we cannot deny it" (Acts 4:16). They then charge Peter and John to keep silence, and let them go free.

Two further miracles, through Peter, are recorded; the healing of a paralysed man at Lydda (Acts 9:32-34), and the raising from death of the widow Tabitha, at Joppa (Acts 9:36-41). In each case the miracle produces many new believers in Jesus the Christ/Messiah (Acts 9:35, 42).

Peter the figure of authority

Peter is shown as having the authority to address certain members of the Jesus-Messiah community, convicting them of deception and wrong-doing. Peter confronts Ananias and his wife Sapphira with their unwillingness (amounting to deception) to share all the profits that they made by selling some property (Acts 5:1-10). Peter tells Ananias that he has lied to God (Acts 5:4), and tells Sapphira that she and her husband had "agreed together to tempt the Spirit of the Lord" (Acts 5:9).[62] Both Ananias and Sapphira fall dead after being found out in their lies and deception. We read that "great fear came upon the whole church, and upon all who heard of these things" (Acts 5:11).

Peter the missionary

Peter becomes a missionary outside the territory of Judea. Following

---

62 See Mt 16:19, where Peter is given the power to "bind" and to "loose."

Philip's success in proclaiming Jesus the Christ to a city of Samaria (Acts 8:4-8), Peter and John go there to pray for those who have been baptized, "that they might receive the Holy Spirit; for it had not yet fallen on any of them, but they had only been baptized in the name of the Lord Jesus" (Acts 8:14-16). Peter has the power/authority to baptize and to be the instrument of the Holy Spirit.

(This Samaritan narrative is the reader's first encounter with the Samaritan Simon – Simon the sorcerer – who tries to buy the gift of the Holy Spirit by offering money to Peter and John (Acts 8:9-11,18-24). In non-canonical writings, Simon the sorcerer reappears in Rome to become one of Simon Peter's strongest adversaries.[63])

Peter the one who brings Gentile believers into communion with 'the circumcised' believers

Acts 10 relates a highly-significant episode - significant not just for the story in Acts, but also for the concern of this present study. Simon Peter is granted a vision (dream?) which readies him to accept that not all that he had thought 'unclean' is in fact 'unclean' (Acts 10:9-16). He is guided to visit the house of a Gentile centurion, Cornelius, where, after Peter has proclaimed the gospel, "the Holy Spirit fell on all who heard the word" (Acts 10:44). These Gentiles begin "speaking in tongues and extolling God" (Acts 10:46). At this, Peter commands that all be baptized "in the name of Jesus Christ" (Acts 10:48).

Later, back in Jerusalem, Peter explains to the brethren (those of the circumcised party) why he went to Cornelius' house, and what had transpired there. "If then God gave the same gift [the Holy Spirit] to them [Gentiles] as he gave to us when we believed in the Lord Jesus Christ, who was I that I could withstand God?" (Acts 11:17).

---

63 From Johnson, *Acts*, 146: "In later Christian writings, the character of Simon is greatly expanded: Justin Martyr, *Apology* 1.26; *Dialogue with Trypho* 120:6; *Acts of Peter* 4-32; Pseudo-Clementine *Homilies* 2, 22-24; Irenaeus, *Against Heresies* 1, 23, all deal with Simon."

Later in Acts it will be Paul who takes the gospel to the wider Gentile world, but according to the author of Acts, it was *Peter* who first met with, and baptised, Gentile believers - thus opening the door to non-Jewish followers of Jesus.

Peter is forced to leave Jerusalem
In Acts 12 there is the first reference to Jacob ('James'), Jesus' brother, and this is in connection with Peter. At some point in the early forties, James of Zebedee is arrested, and beheaded, by order of Herod Agrippa I. Following this, Peter is also arrested and imprisoned (Acts 12:3-4). He miraculously escapes from prison and finds his way back to the house of John Mark's mother (Acts 12:12), and tells the believers gathered there how the Lord had brought him out of prison (Acts 12:17a). Then Peter says: "Tell this to James [Jacob] and to the brethren." At that point Peter left Jerusalem, "and went to another place" (Acts 12:17b).

The author of Acts gives no explanation as who Jacob is, or why Peter should specify that it is Jacob who needs to be informed that Peter has had to leave Jerusalem. However, there appears to be a handing-over to Jacob, Jesus' brother, of the reins of leadership of the Christian Jewish community.

Peter's name
Peter's given name was Simon (or Symeon[64]), yet at some point in his discipleship of Jesus, Jesus gives him the nickname 'Rock' (*Kepha* in the Aramaic, *Petros* in the Greek).[65] As Oscar Cullman says, of *Kepha*:

---

64 Oscar Cullman, *Peter: Disciple, Apostle, Martyr* (New York: Living Age Books, 1958), 17. "The original name of the apostle is Symeon or Simon. Symeon is a Hebrew name much used among the Jews. We find this Semitic form used of Peter, however, only in Acts 15:14 [used by the adult Jacob] and II Peter 1:1."

65 Cullman, *Peter*, 18.

In addition to this name [Symeon/Simon] he has a descriptive title: *Kepha*. This is an Aramaic word and means 'stone', 'rock'. Thus *Kepha* is not, as we might be inclined to think, a proper name. It is not a given name in ordinary use among the Jews, but is rather a common noun. In the New Testament we find this title at times in its Aramaic form, that is, merely *transcribed* in Greek letters; this is usually the case in Paul's letter (Gal 1:18; 2:9; 2:11, 14; 1 Cor 1:12; 3:22; 9:5; 15:5).[66] [Cullman's emphasis]

As for the Greek form, Peter (*Petros*), Cullman says:

According to the Septuagint[67] of Jeremiah 4:29 and Job 30:6, the preferable Greek translation would be *Petra*, which means 'rock'. Since, however, this word is feminine in Greek and has the feminine end –*a*, the New Testament chooses for the translation a less usual Greek word which has the Greek masculine ending -*os*: *Petros* (John 1:42).[68]

Cullman points out something which should be kept in mind:

In order to understand what an impression the giving of a name to Peter must have made on him and on the other witnesses of this event, we would do well to translate the word *Kephas* not with the word Peter, which for us today is all too familiar and has become too rigidly fixed as a proper name, but with the English word 'rock', and so call him Simon Rock.[69]

All four Gospels say that it is Jesus who gives Simon the name 'Rock (*Petros*)' (Mk 3:16, Mt 16:18, Lk 6:14, Jn 1:42). Matthew's Gospel makes it part of a climactic occasion at Caesarea Philippi,

---

66 Cullman, *Peter*, 18.
67 The Greek translation of the Hebrew scriptures.
68 Cullman, *Peter*, 18-19 .
69 Cullman, *Peter*, 20.

when the disciples tell Jesus who people believe he is, and Jesus asks his disciples who *they* believe he is (Mt 16:13-20. When Simon (Peter) says, "You are the Christ, the Son of the Living God" Jesus tells him, "You are Peter (*Petros*), and on this rock (*petra*) I will build my church" (Mt 16:16-18).

Where was Peter in 62 C.E.?

When Jacob died, in Jerusalem, where was Peter? It is possible that Peter was in Jerusalem each year for Passover, and that he could have been there in 62 C.E. Where did Peter go, when he left Jerusalem in the early forties? Acts 12:17b simply says, "Then he departed and went to another place." From Johnson:

> Even leaving aside his role at the apostolic council (Acts 15:7-11), the tradition is unanimous in attributing to Peter a considerable period of travel: Gal 2:14 places him in Antioch; 1 Cor 1:10 and 9:5 offer circumstantial evidence for his having been in Corinth, and a body of testimony supports his ending up in Rome (1 Pet 5:13; *1 Clement* 5:4; *Acts of Peter* 7). The present passage, however, says nothing more than that he removed himself from Jerusalem.[70]

Possible evidence for Peter as a widely-travelled missionary is given in 1 Peter 1:1, which addresses "the exiles of the Dispersion in Pontus, Galatia, Cappadocia, Asia, and Bithynia" (regions encompassed by present-day Turkey) – but did Peter actually visit these areas? The letter is considered by some scholars to be of doubtful authenticity; however, even if not written by Peter himself, the letter names places in which Peter may have preached.[71] In the same letter:

---

[70] Johnson, *Acts*, 214.

[71] From Jerome (c392-393) C.E.: "Simon Peter, the son of John, was from the village of Bethsaida in the province of Galilee, the brother of the apostle Andrew and chief of the apostles. After being bishop of the church in Antioch and preaching to the diaspora of those who had believed in circumcision in Pontus, Galatia, Cappadocia, Asia, and Bithynia, he went

"She who is at Babylon, who is likewise chosen,[72] sends you greetings; and so does my son Mark" (1 Pet 5:13). "Babylon"[73] would seem to be a code-word for Rome, and therefore place the writer of this letter in Rome.

Paul, writing (in about 55-57 C.E.) of his planned visit to the churches in Rome, does not refer to Simon Peter, which is odd if Peter were known to be in Rome at that time. Cullman comments:

> The assertion that he [Paul] purposely refrained from speaking of Peter, because the latter by his Judaizing preaching had worked in Rome in a way contrary to the teaching that Paul set forth in his letter to the Romans, shatters on the already established fact that Peter cannot be called a mere Judaizer; in reality, he stood much closer to the theology of Paul than to that of James [Jacob].[74]

Cullman is well worth reading on this topic of Peter in Rome[75]; however, we are focussing here on whether Simon Peter could have been in Jerusalem in 62 C.E., because my thesis is that he was indeed

---

to Rome in the second year of [the reign of Claudius] to defeat Simon the sorcerer. There he held the priestly chair for twenty-five years, until the final year of Nero's reign, which was year fourteen. He was nailed to a cross by Nero and crowned with martyrdom, with his head turned toward the earth and his feet lifted skyward, for he claimed that he was unworthy of being crucified in the same way as his Lord ... He was buried at Rome on the Vatican Hill, next to the Triumphal Way, and is venerated with honour throughout the whole world." From Jerome's *Illustrious Men* 1,5; in *The Ancient Martyrdom Accounts of Peter and Paul*, David L. Eastman, trans. (Atlanta: SBL Press, 2015), 413.

72 The 'she' who is the 'likewise chosen' is surely Peter's wife. Biblical scholars for some reason prefer to see the 'likewise chosen' as meaning the church in Rome.

73 Ernest Best, *1 Peter* (Grand Rapids, Michigan: William B. Eerdmans/London: Marshall, Morgan & Scott, 1982), 178. "If we take it to signify a real place we find support for this in contemporary and later Judaism which used Babylon as a code name for Rome (2 Baruch 11:1f; 67:7; 2 Esd. 3:1f, 28; *Sibylline Oracles* 5:143, 157ff; it also appears in the Rabbinic literature)."

74 Cullman, *Peter*, 78.

75 Cullman, *Peter*, 70-152.

in Jerusalem at Passover that year, and unwittingly became part of the action leading to Jacob's death.

Peter's death – by crucifixion, or by fire?

It is generally believed that Peter died by crucifixion, and another tradition says that he asked to be crucified upside down.[76] When I came across an article by Timothy D. Barnes, I thought he was onto something significant. Barnes has a different take on the form of Peter's martyrdom: he believes that Peter may have been burned alive, rather than (or as well as being) crucified. After reading Barnes's article, I now believe that there is corroborative evidence for this in John's Gospel. However, this present work concerns Peter as presented in Matthew's Gospel, and it will be on Matthew's narrative of 'the death and redemption of Peter' that we will be focussing.

Matthew's code-words for Simon Peter

petra/petros: *petra* meaning "cliff, crag, rock"; and *petros* meaning "rock, mass, boulder."[77]

***skandalon* (n)**: "stumbling block, a trap, a snare."

***skandalizō* (vb)**: "to cause to stumble, offend, outrage," "to cause to fall into sin."[78]

prōtos: "first"

With these code-words in mind (and the code-words for Jacob) we begin the Gospel, looking for Matthew's hidden story.

---

76 "The Acts of Peter," in *The Other Bible*, Rev. ed., Willis Barnstone, ed. (New York: HarperCollins, 2005), 443.

77 Montanari, Franco, *The Brill Dictionary of Ancient Greek* (Leiden/Boston: Brill, 2015), 1656-7.

78 Montanari, *Dictionary of Ancient Greek*, 1920.

Chapter Four

The genealogy. Matthew 1:1-17

In this work I am proposing that a close study of Matthew's Gospel reveals the Evangelist's highly ambivalent view of Simon Peter: on the one hand Simon Peter is depicted as Jesus' foremost ('first': Mt 10:2) disciple, being given high praise and responsibility by Jesus (Mt 16:17-19), yet on the other hand Matthew seems at times to bring Peter down.[79]

I propose that there is evidence in this Gospel of Matthew's belief that Peter was somehow implicated in the death of Jacob, Jesus' brother, who, in 62 C.E., was thrown from the parapet of the Jerusalem temple sanctuary, then stoned and bashed to death. This execution was carried out on the orders of the high priest and certain members of the Sanhedrin, but I believe Matthew suggests that they were only able to take action against Jacob because of something said to one of them by Peter.

It would seem that the Matthean Evangelist, fearful of undermining the young Christian communities of Jerusalem and further

---

79 See Gundry, Robert H., *Peter: False Disciple and Apostate according to Saint Matthew* (Grand Rapids, Michigan/Cambridge, U.K.: William B. Eerdmans, 2015) and Nau, Arlo, *Peter in Matthew: Discipleship, Diplomacy, and Dispraise* (Collegeville, Minnesota: The Liturgical Press, 1992).

afield, who continued to revere Peter after his death, still needed to record this story - perhaps with the thought that it might come to light at a future time. (There are those enigmatic words put on the lips of Jesus: "for nothing is covered that will not be revealed, or hidden that will not be known" (Mt 10:26).)

These are large claims, but this thesis is not being put forward out of a wish to denigrate Simon Peter, but rather to explore what Matthew seems to be suggesting. Other biblical scholars will be able to assess the validity of what is being put forward in this present work.

The genealogy: Mt 1:1-17

It may seem odd to begin a work focussing on Simon Peter and Jacob, Jesus' brother, with the genealogy of Jesus that Matthew presents in the opening to his Gospel. Yet I propose that not all of the names of those listed in the genealogy are necessarily historical ancestors of Jesus, but through them Matthew is making associations with named and unnamed persons within the body of his narrative of Jesus' life, death, and resurrection.

By this I mean that certain names in this genealogy form a **dramatis personae** - a 'cast list' foreshadowing the people who are part of the story that Matthew tells about Jesus, as well as the Peter-Jacob story that runs like an undercurrent in his Gospel narrative. Jacob was "the brother of the Lord" (Gal 1:19), and is named as such in both Matthew's and Mark's Gospels.[80] This is the Jacob known in his adulthood as 'Jacob the Righteous[81],' who, following

---

80 Mt 13:55; Mk 6:3.

81 Eusebius, *The Ecclesiastical History*, Books I-V, Kirsopp Lake, trans., Loeb Classical Library (Cambridge, Mass./London: Harvard University Press, 1926), 171. Eusebius quotes Hegesippus: "The charge of the Church passed to James [Jacob] the brother of the Lord, together with the Apostles. He was called the 'Just [*dikaios*]' by all men from the Lord's time to ours, since many are called James [Jacob], but he was holy from his mother's womb."

Peter's departure from Jerusalem in the early forties, led the Jewish Christian community until his death in 62 C.E. In other words, Matthew's Gospel is telling both a 'Jesus story' and a 'Peter and Jacob story,' even though these stories are separated in time by some thirty years. Jesus died in about 30 C.E.; Jacob died in 62 C.E.

The first seventeen verses of the Gospel comprise "the genealogy of Jesus Christ, the Son of David, the Son of Abraham" (Mt 1:1). Matthew intentionally gives it in three lists, each (it is claimed) comprising fourteen generations (Mt 1:17).

The first fourteen names give the generations from Abraham, the great patriarch, to "Jesse the father of David the King" (Mt 1:6). The second group of fourteen names lists from David "father of Solomon" to "Josiah the father of Jechoniah and his brothers, at the time of the deportation to Babylon" (Mt 1:11). The third list of fourteen generations (except that there seem to be only thirteen) is from "Jechoniah father of Shealtiel" to "Jacob the father of Joseph the husband of Mary, of whom Jesus was born, who is called Christ" (Mt 1:16).

This genealogy provokes many questions. Why does Matthew list it in three blocks of fourteen generations? Why is the time-scale for each list too great to be covered by fourteen generations?[82] In the first fourteen generations, why is there mention of Judah "and his brothers" (Mt 1:2)? Similarly, in the second fourteen, why the mention of Jechoniah "and his brothers" (Mt 1:11)? Why are three women's names given – Tamar (Mt 1:3), Rahab[83] (Mt 1:5), and Ruth

---

[82] R.T. France, *The Gospel of Matthew* (Grand Rapids, Michigan/Cambridge, U.K.: William B. Eerdmans, 2007), 29. "That Matthew's three fourteens are not simply a matter of historical observation is indicated by the imbalance between the three periods in terms of the actual historical time-scale involved." "It seems then that Matthew's list, like some other biblical genealogies, is selective, and that the scheme of three fourteens is doing something other than recording statistical data."

[83] Frederick Dale Bruner, *Matthew: a commentary*, Rev. ed. (Grand Rapids, Michigan/Cambridge, U.K.: William B. Eerdmans, 2004), 10. "It is hard for the Rahab of the Conquest (and the definite article before the name

(Mt 1:5)? These women were non-Jews, yet according to Matthew each produced a male child who became part of the lineage of the house of Israel.

The genealogical mysteries continue. Solomon's mother is mentioned, but only as "the wife of Uriah" (Mt 1:6b), not by her name, Bathsheba (2 Sam 11:3). Her husband (a Hittite, and therefore a non-Jew) is named, although he has no connection with the house of David.

The names 'Asaph' (Mt 1:7-8) and 'Amos' (Mt 1:10) are given as 'Asa' and 'Amon' in some texts, however, according to scholars, the textual evidence supports the forms 'Asaph' and 'Amos.'[84] There is no known genealogical reason for their inclusion in Matthew's genealogy. Asaph is remembered as a musician in David's court,[85] and Amos was an eight-century prophet.[86] I take it that these are names that Matthew has deliberately chosen, and has not written them through carelessness. Matthew is never careless, never chooses random

---

suggests that she is 'the' Rahab...) to be the mother of Boaz, for she is separated by two hundred years from her Matthean husband (Salmon) and son (Boaz)... But Matthew, who is making a point, does not seem to mind the chronological discrepancy."

84 Raymond E. Brown, *The Birth of the Messiah*, Rev. ed. (New York: Doubleday, 1993), 60. "*Asaph*. This is the best attested reading. Later copyists observed that Matthew's record had confused the psalmist Asaph (title of Pss 50, 73-83; I Chr 16:5-37; II Chr 29:30) with King Asa of Judah (I Kgs 15:9); and so they changed the text to Asa, a reading common in the Byzantine Greek tradition and in the Latin and Syriac versions." Brown, *Birth*, 60-61. "*Amos*. This is the same type of problem as with Asaph/Asa in vs. 7. Later copyists observed that Matthew's record had confused the prophet Amos with King Amon of Judah (II Kgs 21:19); and so they changed the text to Amon."

85 B.T. Dahlberg, "Asaph," in *The Interpreter's Dictionary of the Bible*, Vol. A-D, George Arthur Buttrick, ed. (Nashville: Abingdon Press, 1962), 244-245. "Pss 50; 73-83 contain ascriptions to Asaph in their titles, perhaps indicating a tradition of his authorship of them, or a style peculiar to them and originated by him, or again, perhaps referring simply to the Asaphite guild or to their hymnal."

86 See J.D. Smart, "Amos," in *The Interpreter's Dictionary of the Bible*, Vol. A-D., George Arthur Buttrick, ed. (Nashville: Abingdon Press, 1962), 116-121.

words/names: each name is chosen for its significance in either the 'Jesus story' or the 'Peter-Jacob' story.

The final name in the second list is that of "Jechoniah and his brothers, at the time of the deportation to Babylon" (Mt 1:11), and so the third list resumes "after the deportation." "And after the deportation to Babylon: Jechoniah was the father of Shealtiel, and Shealtiel the father of Zerubbabel, and Zerubbabel the father of Abiud..." (Mt 1:12-13a).

R.T. France comments: "After Zerubbabel Matthew does not trace the royal line through any of the seven sons of Zerubbabel listed in 1 Chr 3:19-20, and we have no information on his source for any of the subsequent names."[87] The list ends with "Jacob the father of Joseph the husband of Mary, of whom Jesus was born, who is called Christ" (Mt 1:16).

We will look closely at these apparent anomalies/oddities, because I am proposing that each of the personalities in the 'Jesus story,' as well as in the hidden 'Peter-Jacob' story,' has a counterpart in the genealogy. Matthew is surely the scribe *par excellence*, who, "trained for the kingdom of heaven is like a householder who brings out of his treasure what is new and what is old" (Mt 13:52). I believe that his love and knowledge of Hebrew scripture is demonstrated in his search to find scriptural 'doubles' (the 'old') for the men and women about whom he writes in the 'Jesus story' and the 'Peter-Jacob story' (the 'new').

Let us take a closer look at these apparent anomalies and oddities in the genealogy, and suggest their counterparts in Matthew's double story.

Judah and his brothers

What is the significance of the words "and his brothers" after Judah's

---

87 France, *Matthew*, 39.

name (Mt 1:2)? Judah was one of the twelve sons of Jacob, and became one of the progenitors of David. Is the phrase "and his brothers" pointing out that these brothers were to become the twelve tribes of Israel?[88] Is it also a reference to the Matthean ideal of community brotherhood, emphasised in this Gospel?[89]

I believe that there is a further reason for this repeated mention of the word 'brother/brothers,' and it is that Matthew has in mind one of the two main players in his hidden story of Simon Peter and Jacob: Jacob and Jesus were **brothers**.

Three women: Tamar, Rahab, Ruth

Tamar (Mt 1:3), Rahab (Mt 1:5) and Ruth (Mt 1:5) are extraordinary names to appear in the genealogy. As others have remarked, we might have expected to see the names of the wives of the patriarchs – women such as Sarah, Rebekah, and Rachel - but not these three women, who were not even Israelites. Why are they included? Rudolf Schnackenburg has a theory which is echoed by others:

> One is struck by the mention of four women: Tamar (v.3), Rahab (v.5a), Ruth (v.5b), and the wife of Uriah (v.6). They are cited not because they were thought of as sinners and probably not because they were foreigners, but because together, through God's providence, they introduce an irregular element into the genealogy. Thereby Matthew prepares us for the altogether extraordinary intervention

---

[88] France, *Matthew*, 35. "The mention of Judah's brothers in v. 2 reflects a natural Jewish interest in the twelve patriarchs from whom the Israelite tribes were named, even though inevitably only one of them can have a place in the genealogy."

[89] Robert H. Gundry, *Matthew: A Commentary on His Handbook for a Mixed Church under Persecution*, 2nd ed. (Grand Rapids, Michigan: William B. Eerdmans, 1994), 14. Gundry says that this reference to 'brothers': "grows primarily out of Matthew's interest in portraying the people of God as a brotherhood ... i.e., Judah and his brothers prefigure the brotherhood of the church."

of God, who willed that the Messiah should be born of the Virgin Mary (Matt. 1:16; 13:55).[90]

Apart from being an "irregular element," the inclusion of these women could be demonstrating 'righteousness,' a theme so important for Matthew. Tamar was "probably a Canaanite (see Genesis 38) and was certainly thought to be so by many Jews in the NT era..."[91] "Her being 'more righteous' than Judah (Gen 38:26) may have contributed to her mention by Matthew, who repeatedly stresses righteousness ..."[92]

Matthew may have had both ideas in mind – the irregular element of the women he has included, as well as the idea of 'righteousness' - in bringing the genealogy to its conclusion with the words "Joseph the husband of Mary of whom Jesus was born" (Mt 1:16). There is no "father of" here – only the fact that Mary is Jesus' mother. It is the righteousness of Joseph, in attending to God's message (through a dream), which leads him to take Mary and her unborn child (of whom he is not the biological father) into a permanent, legal marriage (Mt 1:19-25).

While I take the above into account, I propose that Matthew had a further reason to include these women's names in the genealogy: each is the 'type' of a particular woman in the Matthean narrative that follows. Let us look at each of these three women more closely.

Tamar (Mt 1:3)

Tamar is one of the most interesting women of the Hebrew Bible. She is perhaps best-known for disguising herself as a prostitute in order to seduce her father-in-law Judah and bear him a son (Gen 38:6-30). All takes place as she plans, yet she bears not just one child, but twin

---

90 Rudolf Schnackenburg, *The Gospel of Matthew* (Grand Rapids, Michigan/Cambridge, U.K.: William B. Eerdmans, 2002), 17.

91 Gundry, *Matthew: Commentary*, 14.

92 Gundry, *Matthew: Commentary*, 14.

boys – Perez and Zerah (and Matthew names both, even though it is only Perez who becomes a progenitor of David). Matthew, I believe, is very interested in this story of the birth of these twins – especially the manner of their birth.

> When the time of her delivery came, there were twins in her womb. While she was in labor, one put out a hand; and the midwife took and bound on his hand a crimson thread, saying, "This one came out first." But just then he drew back his hand, and out came his brother; and she said, "What a breach you have made for yourself!" Therefore he was named Perez. Afterward his brother came out with the crimson thread on his hand; and he was named Zerah . (Gen 38:27-30)

Here we have a picture of two boys – twins – struggling to be 'first.' Although Zerah had the crimson thread around his hand, his twin brother Perez actually emerged first, and became the firstborn son, entitled to all the privileges and responsibilities of a firstborn son. When we look at the Matthean 'Jesus story,' there is a mother of two sons (James and John of Zebedee) who is ambitious for her sons to sit on either side of Jesus in his kingdom.

> Then the mother of the sons of Zebedee came up to him, with her sons, and kneeling before him she asked him for something. And he said to her, "What do you want?" She said to him, "Command that these two sons of mine may sit, one at your right hand and one at your left, in your kingdom." (Mt 20:20-21)

The rest of the Twelve react with indignation: "And when the ten heard it, they were indignant at the two brothers" (Mt 20:24). Matthew, by having the mother make the request on her sons' behalf, has softened the account given in Mark's Gospel, which names James and John themselves as seeking the foremost places near Jesus:

> And James and John, the sons of Zebedee, came forward to him, and said to him, "Teacher, we want you to do for

us whatever we ask of you." And he said to them, "What do you want me to do for you?" And they said to him, "Grant us to sit, one at your right hand and one at your left, in your glory." (Mk 10:35-37)

Here the sons themselves are seen as ambitious for the greatest honour – that of sitting either side of Jesus in his kingdom. I am proposing that Matthew, in calling to mind the manner of the birth of Tamar's twins, each struggling for supremacy, is foreshadowing the persons of James and John of Zebedee, two of Jesus' inner circle of the Twelve. But were James and John twins? In Mark's Gospel, Jesus calls the brothers "Boanerges, that is, sons of thunder" (Mk 3:17). I myself had wondered whether "sons of thunder" was a euphemism for 'sons of Zeus/Jupiter.'[93] Might not 'Boanerges' be an allusion to Zeus the god of thunder? Zeus fathered twin sons – Castor and Pollux – from his union with Leda. Are therefore the sons of Zebedee nicknamed "sons of thunder" because they are twins?[94]

Rahab (Mt 1:5)

In Matthew's genealogy Boaz is the son of Rahab and Salmon (Mt 1:5), yet there is a problem with this.

> The reference to Rahab has been added to the genealogical list apparently by Matthew himself (no Rahab is mentioned in the OT lists, which probably serve as source; cf. 1 Chr 2:12; Ruth 4:21). If the Rahab of the conquest narrative is

---

[93] D.E. Nineham, *The Gospel of St Mark* (London: Penguin, 1969), 116-117. " ... if Rendel Harris is right in saying that 'sons of thunder' is closely connected with the cult of twins, the name may have been given because James and John were twins." R.T. France, *The Gospel of Mark* (Grand Rapids, Michigan/ Cambridge, U.K.: William B. Eerdmans, 2002), 162. Footnote 23. "Cf. J.R. Harris' suggestion (*Expositor*, 7th series, 3 [1907] 146-52) that the name refers to the Dioscuri, and was applied to the sons of Zebedee because they were twins."

[94] See Katherine C. Linforth, *The Beloved Disciple: Jacob the Brother of the Lord* (Fremantle, W.A.: VIVID Publishing, 2014), 202, Footnote 386.

in view, as most commentators agree, then Rahab appears several generations, or something like two centuries, too late.[95]

The Gospel 'double' of Rahab is less obvious. Rahab had a reputation both as a prostitute in the city of Jericho and as a friend of the Israelites. In the story told in Joshua 2, she saved two Hebrew spies from capture while they were making reconnaissance in Canaanite territory. In return, she asked for safekeeping for herself and her household, in the event of the city being captured by Joshua's troops. Has Matthew included Rahab as a popular example of a prostitute being justified by her works? From the epistle of James (that is, the adult Jacob), written in the late forties or fifties:

> You see that a man (*anthrōpos* [96]) is justified by works and not by faith alone. And in the same way was not also Rahab the harlot justified by works when she received the messengers and sent them out another way? (Jas 2:24-25)[97]

The letter to the Hebrews also speaks of Rahab's righteousness:

> By faith Rahab the harlot did not perish with those who were disobedient, because she had given friendly welcome to the spies. (Heb 11:31)

Who, in Matthew's narrative, would be foreshadowed by the figure of Rahab the prostitute? Matthew never identifies a prostitute as such, yet it seems likely that Rahab prefigures the woman who anointed Jesus at Bethany (Mt 26:6-7; cf. Mk 14:3; Lk 7:36-38; Jn 12:1-3). In Matthew's Gospel the woman comes to Jesus while he is in the house of Simon the leper, and anoints Jesus' head with "very expensive ointment" (Mt 26:7). The indignant disciples complain about

---

95 Donald A. Hagner, *Matthew 1-13* (Dallas, Texas: Word Books, c1993), 11.

96 Unfortunately *anthrōpos* has a history of being translated as 'man,' whereas the real meaning is 'human being.'

97 'James' is Jacob (Gk: *Iakōbos*), the brother of Jesus. See Luke Timothy Johnson, *The letter of James* (New York: Doubleday, 1995), 92-93.

what they see as a waste of money – money which could have helped the poor. Jesus responds:

> Why do you trouble the woman? For she has done a beautiful thing to me. For you always have the poor with you, but you will not always have me. In pouring this ointment on my body she has done it to prepare me for burial. Truly, I say to you, wherever this gospel is preached in the whole world, what she has done will be told in memory of her (Mt 26:10-13).

The passage in Mark's Gospel has a similar ending (Mk 14:6-9). But why does neither Evangelist name the woman? What she has done for Jesus will "be told in memory of her," but her name is not given.

Similarly, in Luke's Gospel, the woman who anoints Jesus is not named, but she is described as "a woman of the city, who was a sinner" (Lk 7:37). The woman wets Jesus' feet with her tears, then dries them with her hair. She then takes a flask of ointment and anoints his feet. Luke develops this episode into a dialogue between Jesus and the Pharisees, concerning love and forgiveness (Lk 7:39-50). The woman's actions therefore become, in Luke's hands, a platform for teaching, rather than something for which she is to be remembered "wherever this gospel is preached in the whole world."[98]

John's Gospel gives a different version of the anointing (Jn 12:1-3), and here the woman is Mary (Mary of Bethany, sister of Martha and Lazarus; Jn 11:1-2). As in the Lukan episode, the woman, Mary, anoints Jesus' feet and wipes them with her hair. There is a protest, from Judas Iscariot, about the amount of money used to

---

98 France, *Matthew*, 973. "The anonymity of this woman in Matthew and Mark is the more remarkable in that her deed is to be a perpetual memorial to her (v. 13). She is to be remembered, but she has no name!" According to France (p. 973, Footnote 7) the 4th-century Ephraem is the first known writer to put forward that this woman is Mary Magdalene.

buy the ointment - money which could have been given to the poor. Jesus' response is: "The poor you always have with you, but you do not always have me" (Jn 12:8).

In the history of the teaching of the Catholic Church, this anointing woman was understood to be Mary Magdalene – a repentant and reformed prostitute. This teaching has been rescinded, yet I believe the Church's original thinking was correct. In my book, *The Beloved Disciple: Jacob the Brother of the Lord*, I come to the conclusion that, in John's deeply symbolic Gospel, 'Mary of Bethany' is based on Mary Magdalene.[99] ('Martha' represents Jesus' and Jacob's mother Mary, and 'Lazarus' represents Jesus' brother Jacob.) If the anointing woman is the same woman in all four Gospels, then she is Mary Magdalene, and most probably a former prostitute (Luke's "woman of the city, who was a sinner"; Lk 7:37), or at least a woman of easy virtue.

Concerning Mary Magdalene, Luke says: "And the twelve were with him [Jesus], and also some women who had been healed of evil spirits and infirmities: Mary, called Magdalene, from whom seven demons had gone out..." (Lk 8:1-2). While there is no specific mention of prostitution, we are left to wonder about the "seven demons."[100]

I believe that, in John's Gospel, the woman of Samaria (as with 'Mary of Bethany') is also Mary Magdalene.[101] There is an interesting conversation between Jesus and the Samaritan woman, concerning her relationships with men:

Jesus said to her, "Go, call your husband, and come here."

The woman answered him, "I have no husband." Jesus said

---

[99] Linforth, *Beloved Disciple*, 121-122.

[100] Joseph A. Fitzmyer, *The Gospel according to Luke I-IX* (New York: Doubleday, 1979), 697-698. "*Out of whom seven demons had come*. I.e. through an exorcism, presumably performed by Jesus. The number of the demons is supposed to imply the severity of the possession."

[101] Linforth, *Beloved Disciple*, 250-262.

to her, "You are right in saying, 'I have no husband'; for you have had five husbands, and he whom you now have is not your husband; this you said truly." The woman said to him, "Sir, I perceive that you are a prophet." (Jn 4:16-19)

The conventional explanation of the "five husbands" is that this is meant allegorically – that Samaria had worshipped, in its time, at least five gods.[102] Otherwise one takes this saying (that the woman has had five husbands) at face value: she has been married five times. But is John being deliberately ambiguous here? Were the five husbands really husbands of this woman, or did the Samaritan woman have sexual relationships with the husbands of five other women? The words "he whom you have now is not your husband" could imply this. Most probably this present man is also the husband of some other woman. How many men in a Semitic community would still be unmarried in adulthood?

With this in mind – that Mary Magdalene was the anointing woman, and a former prostitute – the words of Jesus to the chief priests and elders, concerning tax collectors (Matthew) and prostitutes (Mary Magdalene) have a real resonance:

> Truly, I say to you, the tax collectors and the harlots go into the kingdom of God before you. For John came to you in the way of righteousness, and you did not believe him, but the tax collectors and the harlots believed him; and even when you saw it, you did not afterward repent and believe him. (Mt 21:31b-32)

We hear of Matthew the tax collector leaving everything and following Jesus (Mt 9:9)[103], but does the Evangelist have a story of a

---

102 Raymond E. Brown, *The Gospel according to John. I-XII*, 2nd ed. (New York: Doubleday, 1986), 171.

103 Mt 9:9. "As Jesus passed on from there, he saw a man called Matthew sitting at the tax office; and he said to him, 'Follow me.' And he rose and followed him."

prostitute doing likewise? Matthew is silent on this. Was it indeed Mary Magdalene, who was a former prostitute, and was still alive (or who had died but whose memory and name were revered) when Matthew was writing? He could have believed it necessary to omit her name: it would have been an embarrassment that one so close to Jesus could have once been a prostitute, or at the very least a 'loose woman.'

I believe that Mary Magdalene is foreshadowed by Rahab in Matthew's genealogy.

Ruth (Mt 1:5)

In the book of Ruth, Ruth (a non-Israelite) is recorded as marrying and bearing a son to a Jewish man, Boaz. The child is Obed, who will become the father of Jesse, who will become the father of David (Ruth 4:13-17). Ruth thus joins Tamar and Rahab as a non-Israelite woman whose son enters the lineage of the house of David.[104]

The story of Ruth is well-known. She was a widow, who left her home country of Moab to accompany her widowed mother-in-law Naomi to Naomi's homeplace of Bethlehem in Judea. It is in the fields outside Bethlehem (fields belonging to Naomi's kinsman Boaz) that Ruth undertakes to glean behind the harvesters, picking up dropped ears of corn with which to feed Naomi and herself. Boaz is informed by his harvesters of Ruth's identity, and why she is gleaning. Rather than forbidding her to glean, Boaz orders his harvesters to let her keep gleaning. He goes further: the harvesters are directed to make sure that Ruth is not molested, that she has water to drink, and that she be allowed to glean right behind Boaz' harvesters. In fact, the harvesters are to pull out some corn from the bundles and drop it, so that Ruth has even more corn to gather up (Ruth 2:1-16).

---

[104] W.D. Davies and Dale C. Allison, *A Critical and Exegetical Commentary on the Gospel according to Saint Matthew*, Vol. 1, Matthew I-VII (London/ New York: T&T Clark, 2004), 173-174. "Rabbinic tradition made her a proselyte, the mother of kings, and an ancestress of the Messiah ... "

I trace the outline of the foreign-born Ruth behind the figure of the Canaanite woman of Matthew's Gospel, who comes to plead with Jesus and his disciples to have her daughter released from the power of a demon (Mt 15:21-28). The question arises – why does Matthew describe the woman as a Canaanite (cf. Mk 7:26, where the woman is Syrophoenician)? Davies and Allison give six possible reasons for this; however they regard (as I do) the sixth explanation as the most satisfactory:

> Most modern exegetes have supposed the change to 'Canaanite' was made because of its OT associations: one automatically thinks of Israel's enemies. Thereby is invoked 'Israel's deeply-ingrained fear of, and revulsion towards Gentile ways' ... which in turn allows one to see in Jesus the overcoming of such fear and revulsion.[105]

What are the similarities between Ruth and the Canaanite woman? Both women are aliens, non-Israelites, of peoples traditionally hostile to Israel. Ruth is from Moab (Ruth 1:4) and the woman with the afflicted daughter is a Canaanite from the region of Tyre and Sidon (Mt 15:21-22).

Both women leave their own home territory, and meet a man (someone who will help them) coming out from his own region. Boaz comes out from Bethlehem (Ruth 2:4), and Jesus "withdraws" to the district of Tyre and Sidon (Mt 15:21-22).

Both women make obeisance to the man. Ruth makes obeisance to Boaz: "Then she fell prostrate, with her face to the ground, and said to him, 'Why have I found favor in your sight, that you should take notice of me, when I am a foreigner?'" (Ruth 2:10). Similarly, the Canaanite woman makes obeisance to Jesus. "But she came and knelt before him, saying 'Lord, help me'" (Mt 15:25).

---

105 W.D. Davies and Dale C. Allison, *A Critical and Exegetical Commentary on the Gospel according to Saint Matthew*, Vol. 2, Matthew VIII-XVIII (London/New York: T&T Clark, 2004), 547.

In the story of Ruth, Boaz orders his harvesters to take every care that Ruth is both protected and allowed to gather as much corn as she can. There is to be no stinting. However, in the case of the Canaanite woman, Jesus' disciples (his 'harvesters') do not remember (or do not heed) his words spoken earlier to them: "The harvest is plentiful, but the laborers are few; pray therefore the Lord of the harvest to send out laborers into his harvest" (Mt 9:37b-38). The disciples do not know how to act, when the woman follows them and calls out to them. Their response to Jesus is, "Send her away, for she is crying after us" (Mt 15:23).

Has Matthew, born teacher than he is, included Ruth in the genealogy, so that later on, with the story of the Canaanite woman, the message can be driven home that foreigners, in Israel's history, have been welcomed and looked after, and been incorporated into the house of Israel? The Canaanite woman is seeking something which the disciples could, and should, be helping her find. Ruth thus becomes a teaching model for Matthew's church community: the community should be welcoming those non-Jews who approach, seeking Jesus, and who may eventually become part of that community.

Ruth thus foreshadows the Canaanite woman of the Gospel.

The wife of Uriah (Mt 1:6)

The second fourteen generations of the genealogy, which take us from David's kingship to the time of the deportation to Babylon, record yet another woman - well-known, yet here unnamed. "And David was the father of Solomon by the wife of Uriah" (Mt 1:6b). The story of David's seduction of the wife of Uriah, the Hittite commander in David's army, is one of the most well-known in Hebrew scripture. David, from his palace rooftop, sees a beautiful woman bathing, and enquires who she is. He is told "This is Bathsheba daughter of Eliam, the wife of Uriah the Hittite" (2 Sam 11:3).

Most readers of Matthew's Gospel would know that it is Bathsheba who is the wife of Uriah, yet she is not named in the genealogy.

Why not? It is because Matthew's focus here is on Uriah, who was not an Israelite but he held a high post in David's army. Who in Matthew's 'Jesus story' could be seen as a sort of 'double'? When we read the David/Bathsheba/Uriah story we begin to see a connection.

After King David secretly meets with Bathsheba, while Uriah and his men are away fighting, Bathsheba falls pregnant to David. Attempting to conceal his part in this pregnancy, David has Uriah recalled from the battlefield back to Jerusalem, and tries to get him to go home to Bathsheba. The unspoken plan is that Uriah will have sexual relations with his wife, and accept the subsequent child as his own. Uriah, however, refuses to go back to the comfort of his own home and wife, and, when questioned by David as to why he doesn't do so, replies:

> The ark and Israel and Judah remain in booths; and my lord Joab and the servants of my lord are camping in the open field; shall I then go to my house, to eat and to drink, and to lie with my wife? As you live, and as your soul lives, I will not do such a thing. (2 Sam 11:11)

David tries again, the next day, by getting Uriah well-fed, and drunk; however Uriah "did not go down to his house" (2 Sam 11:12-13).

Thus we know that Uriah is a man of integrity, who will not return to the comforts of his home and wife while his troops are still on the battlefield. Do we then see a 'double' for Uriah in the person of the centurion (a non-Jew) who comes to Jesus, asking for help for his servant, who is paralysed and "in terrible distress" (Mt 8:6)? The centurion describes himself as "a man under authority, with soldiers under me" (Mt 8:9). His concern for the welfare of his servant reflects the concern which Uriah had for his troops. The centurion could not – would not – ignore his servant's plight at his own expense.

I believe that Uriah the Hittite foreshadows the Gentile centurion in Matthew's Gospel.

Asaph (Mt 1:7-8) and Amon (Mt 1:10)

The generations continue: "Solomon the father of Rehoboam, and Rehoboam the father of Abijah, and Abijah the father of Asa" (as listed in 1 Chronicles 3:10). In Matthew 1:7-8, however, some authorities have 'Asaph' instead of 'Asa.' Some scholars see this as confusion on Matthew's part.[106] I believe, however, that Matthew deliberately writes 'Asaph.' Asaph was a musician in the court of David, and various psalms (Pss 50, 73-83) are attributed either to him or to the music guild in his name. Gundry notes the tradition that Psalm 78 is ascribed to Asaph, and that "In 13:35 Matthew will quote part of that psalm as fulfilled. Thus a note of prophecy comes into the genealogy."[107]

> This was to fulfil what was spoken by the prophet: "I will open my mouth in parables, I will utter what has been hidden from the foundation." [RSV adds "of the world"] (Mt 13:35)

There is a similar situation with the name Amos (Mt 1:10), sometimes written as 'Amon' (from the listing in 1 Chr 3:14), and I agree with Gundry:

> But Matthew may have chosen or coined the spelling 'Amos' for a secondary allusion to the prophet Amos, just as he spelled Asa's name like that of Asaph to introduce a prophetic note. In support of this possibility, Matthew's version of Jesus' saying recorded in 10:29 and worded differently in Luke 12:6 conforms to Amos 3:5.[108]

We will look at Matthew 10:29 later, within the context of Matthew's 'Peter-Jacob story.'

---

106 Davies and Allison, *Saint Matthew*, 1:175.
107 Gundry, *Matthew: Commentary*, 15.
108 Gundry, *Matthew: Commentary*, 16.

The Deportation

The second list of fourteen generations ends with "Josiah the father of Jechoniah and his brothers, at the time of the deportation to Babylon" (Mt 1:11). There is difficulty with this statement, because Jechoniah was not the son of Josiah, but of Jehoiakim.[109] Why then has Matthew used the name 'Jechoniah'? We need to read the relevant passage in 1 Chronicles to learn more about Jechoniah. Jechoniah had a brother, Zedekiah (1 Chr 3:16), and Jechoniah is described as "Jechoniah the captive" (1 Chr 3:17).[110]

I believe that Matthew has deliberately chosen the name Jechoniah instead of Jehoiachim for two reasons: first, because Jechoniah is described as "the captive," and second, Jechoniah's (presumably younger) brother is named Zedekiah (which means 'God is my righteousness'[111]). Let us assume that with "Jechoniah the captive" Matthew is finding a scriptural type to represent Jesus at the time of his arrest and execution (his captivity). The 'deportation' is thus a foreshadowing of Jesus' death and departure from this world, and 'after the deportation' foreshadows post-c30 C.E., when the Christian Jewish community of Jerusalem was led first by Peter, then by Jacob. Simon Peter was leader of the Jerusalem Christian community until some time in the early forties (Acts 12:17); then Jacob, Jesus' younger brother, took on the leadership until his death in 62 C.E.

Matthew makes 'the deportation' a feature of this genealogy. As Nicholas G. Piotrowski writes:

> It is [also] worth pointing out that 'the deportation' is the only event –other than constant 'begetting' – *explicitly* mentioned in the genealogy. Without mention of the

---

109 Hagner, *Matthew 1-13*, 6.
110 Davies and Allison, *Saint Matthew*, 1:178.
111 H.B. MacLean, "Zedekiah," in *The Interpreter's Dictionary of the Bible*, Vol. R-Z, George Arthur Buttrick, ed. (Nashville: Abingdon Press, 1962), 947. "Yahu is (my) righteousness."

historic return, this 'deportation' is quite peculiar to the reader. It breaks up the structure anticipated by v. 1 and is the only explicit event in an otherwise list of names.[112] [Piotrowski's emphasis]

Piotrowski says further:

Moreover, the reader [also] observes that this deportation/beginning of exile marks the end of the Davidic dynasty, and that it is the only event in the entire history of Israel that is explicitly referenced (four times in fact in vv. 11-12, 17). But *the return is nowhere mentioned*. The μετοικεσια, therefore, is Matthew's '*crux historiae* in the story of the nation,' the defining mark for the end of the Davidic monarchy. Without mention of a return or re-enthronement of the House of David, the entire third table of the genealogy comprises the time μετα ... τεν μετοικεσιαν, the time in Israel's history without a Davidic king. Thus, in *Matthew's narrative world*, the exile – begun with 'the deportation' – has not come to a satisfying conclusion insofar as the Davidic throne remains vacant.[113] [Piotrowski's emphases]

I believe that the list of names "after the deportation" (starting from Shealtiel and ending with Joseph (Mt 1:12-16) represents ten of the Twelve chosen by Jesus to be his closest disciples, and who continued in that role after his death and resurrection. The list also contains a 'type' for Jacob, Jesus' brother, who was not one of the Twelve, but who became their leader from the early forties.

---

112 Nicholas G. Piotrowski, "'After the Deportation': Observations in Matthew's apocalyptic genealogy," in *Bulletin for Biblical Research* 25:2 (2015), 193-4.

113 Piotrowski, "After the Deportation," 196.

The Twelve

I can see no direct correspondence in Matthew's third list of names (Mt 1:12-16) with the names of ten of the Twelve in Matthew's Gospel (Mt 10:2-4), except in the case of two of them (with a possible third). If we exclude Joseph, then we have ten names, in the centre of which is the name 'Zadok.' Shealtiel, Zerubbabel, Abiud, Eliakim, and Azor come before the name Zadok; Achim, Eliud, Eleazar, Matthan, and Jacob follow the name Zadok. We identified James and John of Zebedee earlier, in the persons of the twins Perez and Zerah, and this has left us with ten of the Twelve centred around Zadok. Zadok (that is, 'the righteous one,' who is Jacob the brother of Jesus) is the central, most important person in the group – as the leader he was, from the early forties until his death.

Judas Iscariot died by his own hand, according to Matthew, even before Jesus was put to death (Mt 27:3-5). However, according to Acts, Matthias was chosen to fill the vacancy left by Judas, to complete the Twelve. It may be, then, that the 'Matthan' of Mt 1:15 is to be equated with the Matthias of Acts 1:21-26.

Simon Peter

The name Eliakim (Mt 1:13), I believe, has been chosen by Matthew as Simon Peter's 'double.' In Matthew 16:19 Jesus says to Peter: "I will give you the keys of the kingdom of heaven, and whatever you bind on earth shall be bound in heaven, and whatever you loose on earth shall be loosed in heaven ..." This promise is an echo of a promise made to Eliakim, who was to replace Shebna, the steward of the royal household (Isa 22:20-22). Eliakim was royal chamberlain to King Hezekiah, and therefore had power "second only to the king."[114]

On that day I will call my servant Eliakim son of Hilkiah,

---

114 J. M. Ward, "Eliakim," in *The Interpreter's Dictionary of the Bible*, Vol. E-J, George Arthur Buttrick, ed. (Nashville: Abingdon, 1962), 86.

and will clothe him with your robe and bind your sash on him. I will commit your authority to his hand, and he shall be a father to the inhabitants of Jerusalem and to the house of Judah. I will place on his shoulder the key of the house of David; he shall open, and no one shall shut; he shall shut, and no one shall open. (Isa 22:20-22)

I see Eliakim as the character in the genealogy who foreshadows Simon Peter, in Matthew's Gospel.

Jacob the brother of Jesus

Centrally-placed (denoting his significance as Jesus' brother, and as the leader of the Christian Jewish movement in Jerusalem and elsewhere) among the ten names from Shealtiel to Jacob is the name Zadok, which means, in Hebrew, 'righteous one.' I believe this to be Matthew's way of referencing Jesus' brother -'Jacob the Righteous.' Eusebius quotes Hegesippus (of "the generation after the Apostles"[115]) as speaking of Jacob as 'righteous.' Eusebius also quotes from Clement of Alexandria, concerning Jacob:

> Peter and James [of Zebedee] and John after the Ascension of the Saviour did not struggle for glory, because they had previously been given honour by the Saviour, but chose James the Just [*Iakōbon ton dikaion*] as Bishop of Jerusalem.[116]

> After the Resurrection the Lord gave the tradition of knowledge to James the Just [*Iakōbo tō dikaiō*] and John and Peter, these gave it to the other Apostles and the other Apostles to the seventy, of whom Barnabas also was one. Now there were two Jameses (*Iakōboi*), one James the Just (*dikaios*), who was thrown down from the pinnacle of the

---

115 Eusebius, *Ecclesiastical History* (2.23), 171.
116 Eusebius, *Ecclesiastical History* (2.1), 105.

temple and beaten to death with a fuller's club, and the other he who was beheaded.[117]

Conclusion

The first seventeen verses of Matthew's Gospel have baffled scholars, setting them a puzzle they are determined to resolve. In the genealogical lists there are very obvious omissions of names; there are also additional names which are not recorded in any other genealogical listing. Most unexpected are the names of three women, and another who is 'the wife of Uriah.'

The phrase 'his brothers' features twice, a forerunner of the emphasis Matthew will place on 'brother' in the body of his Gospel. The brotherhood of the Christian Jewish community is certainly of enormous concern for Matthew, yet I believe the word ' brother' is, at times, a definite pointer to Jacob, the brother of Jesus.

I have drawn attention to many of the names in the genealogy, which together comprise a *dramatis personae* – a 'cast list' of those who make an appearance in Matthew's Gospel. Matthew will write the story of Jesus, but he will also write the hidden story of Jesus' brother, Jacob, and Peter, the 'first' of the Twelve.

---

117 Eusebius, *Ecclesiastical History* (2.1), 105.

Chapter Five

The temptations. Matthew 4:1-11

We now enter the body of Matthew's story, following on from the genealogy, the infancy narrative, and the baptism of Jesus by John the Baptist. We pick up the narrative when Jesus has been led by the Spirit into the wilderness, where three times the devil offers him temptations.

We need to keep in mind the fact that this Gospel was written (completed?) after the death of Jesus' brother Jacob, which took place in 62 C.E.[118] For Matthew, the event must have been shattering. Matthew's Gospel is the most 'Jewish' of the three Synoptic Gospels - heavily referencing the fulfilment of the Hebrew scriptures, and emphasising the necessity of keeping the Mosaic Law. The death of Jacob the Righteous ('James the Just'), the leader of the Christian Jewish movement, must have had a profound effect on all - not only on the Christian Jews but also on the Jews who respected Jacob for his commitment to Jewish Law. This evidenced in Josephus' account of the public reaction to Jacob's death.[119]

---

118 W.D. Davies and Dale C. Allison, *A Critical and Exegetical Commentary on the Gospel according to Saint Matthew*, Vol. 1, Matthew I-VII (London/New York: T&T Clark, 2004), 138: "To sum up: Matthew was almost certainly written between A.D. 70 and A.D. 100, in all probability between A.D. 80 and 95." [I would date its completion as post-70 but pre-80.]

119 Josephus, *Jewish Antiquities*, Books XVIII-XX, Louis H. Feldman, trans.,

In Matthew's account of the devil's tempting of Jesus in the desert, I believe there is an allusion to Jacob's death, which is not found in Mark's account of the temptations. Mark's Gospel is generally taken to be the earliest written Gospel, and it would seem that Matthew elaborated on Mark's account, in significant ways.[120] Mark says simply: "The Spirit immediately drove him [Jesus] out into the wilderness. And he was in the wilderness forty days, tempted by Satan; and he was with the wild beasts; and the angels ministered to him" (Mk 1:12-13).

The first temptation. Matthew 4:1-4

As with Luke (Lk 4:1-13), Matthew elaborates on Mark's account, regarding the number and nature of the temptations. The first temptation is for Jesus to provide food for himself, by turning the stones of the desert into loaves of bread.

Then Jesus was led up by the Spirit into the wilderness to be tempted by the devil (diabolos). And he fasted forty days and forty nights, and afterward he was hungry. And the tempter came and said to him, "If you are the Son of God, command these stones (lithoi) to become loaves of bread." But he answered, "It is written, 'Man shall not

---

Loeb Classical Library (London: William Heinemann/Cambridge, Mass.: Harvard University Press, 1965), 495, 497. "... Ananus [high priest] thought that he had a favourable opportunity because Festus [the Roman procurator] was dead and Albinus was still on the way. And so he convened the judges of the Sanhedrin and brought before them a man named James [Jacob], the brother of Jesus who was called the Christ, and certain others. He accused them of having transgressed the law and delivered them up to be stoned. Those of the inhabitants of the city [Jerusalem] who were considered the most fair-minded and who were in strict observance of the law were offended at this. They therefore secretly sent to King Agrippa urging him, for Ananus had not even been correct in his first step, to order him to desist from any further such actions."

120 Donald A. Hagner, *Matthew 1-13* (Dallas, Texas: Word:Books, c1993), xlvii. " It is [also] the case that in the vast majority of instances, it is easier to explain why and how Matthew may have redacted Mark than vice versa."

> live by bread alone, but by every word that proceeds from the mouth of God.'" (Mt 4:1-4)

Here we have the first reference in Mathew's Gospel to the devil (*diabolos*), who appears here in the desert as 'the tempter' (*peirazōn*). There is also the first reference in the Gospel to stones (*lithoi*) – stones which the devil urges Jesus to turn into loaves of bread. The temptation is not just to create food to eat, but to demonstrate that Jesus, as Son of God, has the power to work a miracle to his own advantage. These stones in the desert are not stones to trip over, but metaphorically they have the potential to cause Jesus to 'trip.' Jesus responds to the devil by quoting scripture: "Man shall not live by bread alone, but by every word that proceeds from the mouth of God" (Deut 8:3).

We note the mention of 'stones (*lithoi*)' in this first temptation, but it is the second temptation which is the most significant in Matthew's narrative, in regard to the death of Jacob.

The second temptation. Matthew 4:5-7

> Then the devil (*diabolos*) took him to the holy city and set him (*estēsen auton*) on the pinnacle (pterugion = 'little wing") of the temple, and said to him, "If you are the Son of God, throw (*balē*) yourself down; for it is written, 'He will give his angels charge of you,' and 'On their hands they will bear you up, lest you strike your foot against a stone (*pros lithon*) .'" Jesus said to him, "Again it is written, 'You shall not tempt the Lord your God'[121]." (Mt 4:5-7)

This image of Jesus, possibly 'throwing' himself from the little wing of the temple, must have been confronting for those many Gospel readers/listeners who remembered how Jacob died. It was Jesus' own brother who was publicly executed in Jerusalem – an event

---

121 Deut 6:16.

that occurred little more than twenty years before Matthew completed his Gospel. Jacob's death would have been indelibly imprinted in Matthew's mind – either from Matthew having witnessed it, or having been told about it. We have accounts of Jacob's death from various sources, which tell of Jacob having been thrown from a high point (*pterugion* = 'little wing') of the temple.

From The Second Apocalypse of James, we read:

> And I was with the priests and revealed nothing of the relationship, since all of them were saying with one voice, "Come, let us stone the Just One." And they arose, saying, "Yes, let us kill this man, that he may be taken from our midst. For he will be of no use to us." And they were there and found him standing beside the columns of the temple beside the mighty corner stone. And they decided to throw him down from the height, and they cast him down ...
>
> They seized him and [struck] him as they dragged him upon the ground. They stretched him out, and placed a stone on his abdomen. They all placed their feet on him, saying, "You have erred!" Again they raised him up, since he was alive, and made him dig a hole. They made him stand in it. After having covered him up to his abdomen, they stoned him in this manner.[122]

Hegesippus (2nd century historian) also wrote an account of the death of Jacob:

> Now, since many even of the rulers believed, there was a tumult of the Jews and the Scribes and the Pharisees saying that the whole people was in danger of looking for Jesus as the Christ. So they assembled and said to James [Jacob], "We beseech you to restrain the people since they are straying

---

122 Charles W. Hendrick, "The (Second) Apocalypse of James," in *The Nag Hammadi Library in English*, 3rd rev. ed., James M. Robinson, ed. (New York: HarperSanFrancisco, 1990), 275.

after Jesus as though he were the Messiah. We beseech you to persuade concerning Jesus all who come for the day of the Passover, for all obey you. For we and the whole people testify to you that you are righteous and do not respect persons. So do you persuade the crowd not to err concerning Jesus, for the whole people and we all obey you. Therefore stand on the battlement (*pterugion tou hierou*) of the temple that you may be clearly visible on high, and that your words may be audible to all the people, for because of the Passover all the tribes, with the Gentiles also, have come together." So the Scribes and Pharisees mentioned before made James [Jacob] stand on the battlement of the temple (*pterugion tou naou*), and they cried out to him and said, "Oh, just one to whom we all owe obedience, since the people are straying after Jesus who was crucified, tell us what is the gate of Jesus?" And he answered with a loud voice, "Why do you ask me concerning the Son of Man? He is sitting in heaven on the right hand of the great power, and he will come on the clouds of heaven." And many were convinced and confessed at the testimony of James [Jacob] and said, "Hosanna to the Son of David." Then again the same Scribes and Pharisees said to one another, "We did wrong to provide Jesus with such testimony, but let us go up and throw him down that they may be afraid and not believe him." And they cried out saying, "Oh, oh, even the just one erred." And they fulfilled the Scripture written in Isaiah, "Let us take the just man for he is unprofitable to us. Yet they shall eat the fruit of their works." So they went up and threw down the Just, and they said to one another, "Let us stone James the Just (*Iakōbon ton dikaion*)," and they began to stone him since the fall had not killed him, but he turned and knelt saying, "I beseech thee, O Lord, God and Father, forgive them, for they know not what they do." And while they were thus stoning him one of the priests of the sons of Rechab, the son of Rechabim, to whom Jeremiah the prophet bore witness, cried out saying, "Stop! What are you doing? The Just is praying for you." And a certain man among them, one of the laundrymen, took the club with which he used to beat out the clothes, and hit the Just and so he suffered martyrdom. And they buried him on the spot by the temple (*para to nao*), and his gravestone still remains by the temple (*para to nao*). [123]

In the same way that Jacob was taken by his enemies up to the 'little wing' of the temple, the Matthean Jesus is taken up by the devil and set on the 'little wing' of the temple, where he is invited to throw himself down ("If you are the Son of God ..."). Matthew is surely recalling Jacob's death, in his depiction of this particular temptation which the devil presents to Jesus.

The little wing (*pterugion*) of the temple

Where was the 'little wing' of the Temple? Was it part of the sanctuary proper (naos), or part of the larger temple complex (*hieros*)? The accounts in Matthew and Luke use the word *hieros* (Mt 4:5; Lk 4:9), which would imply the wider sense of the word 'temple.' Hegesippus's account moves between *hieros* (the temple complex as a whole) and *naos* (the sanctuary itself).

R.T. France translates *pterugion* as 'high corner':

Apart from the parallel in Luke (and subsequent Christian references to this passage) the word is not used elsewhere of a building feature, though there are rare uses of it in classical literature for a projecting piece of a coat of armor or of a rudder or other machinery. The context makes it

---

123 Eusebius, *The Ecclesiastical History*, Books I-V (2.23), Kirsopp Lake, trans., Loeb Classical Library (Cambridge, Mass./London: Harvard University Press, 1926), 173, 175.

clear only that it is a high part of the temple from which a fall might be expected to be fatal. This might either be a part of the sanctuary building itself (which was some fifty meters high) or perhaps of the temple's outer portico, which on the east overhung the deep Kidron valley."[124]

Hegesippus says that Jacob was thrown from a high point of the sanctuary (*naos*) itself, not from the south-east corner of the outer wall.

Matthew says that the devil took Jesus to Jerusalem (the holy city) and "set him (*estēsen auton*)" on the little wing of the temple. "Set him"[125] implies an act of deliberately placing something or someone in a certain position or place. Matthew could simply have said that the devil took Jesus to the wing of the temple – leaving out the "set him" phrase. With the phrase "set him" we have a mental image of the devil forcibly setting Jesus into place on the wing of the temple. In the same way, Jacob was forced by his adversaries to stand on the wing of the temple, before being thrown to his death.

Stone/stones (*lithos/lithoi*)

In tempting Jesus, the devil quotes from Psalm 91:11-12:

'He will give his angels charge of you,' and 'On their hands they will bear you up, lest you strike your foot against a stone (*pro lithon*).' (Mt 4:6)

The Septuagint[126] reading says: "For he shall give his angels charge concerning thee, to keep thee in all thy ways. They shall bear thee up on their hands, lest at any time thou dash thy foot against

---

124 R.T. France, *The Gospel of Matthew* (Grand Rapids, Michigan/Cambridge, U.K.: William B. Eerdmans, 2007), 132.

125 Vb *histēmi*. 'stand,' make stand,' 'place.'

126 The Septuagint is a Greek translation of the Hebrew scriptures, compiled possibly between the third and first centuries B.C.E..

a stone."[127] Matthew omits "in all your ways" because the emphasis here is on the one particular situation of throwing one's self from the little wing of the temple. Furthermore, Matthew has used the temple as a location for this scene, yet the accompanying quotation from scripture has no reference to a temple location or even a high building. So it seems that Matthew 4:6 is the Evangelist's creative use of Hebrew scripture.

The psalm in its original form does not describe someone falling (much less throwing themselves) from a height, but as Robert H. Gundry says, it implies someone tripping over, or stumbling, because of a stone in his/her path.[128] Yet the devil tells Jesus to throw himself down from the wing of the temple, and (if he is the Son of God) the angels will bear him up and prevent him from being dashed on the stones below.

It is not credible that Matthew did not have Jacob's death in mind while writing down this particular temptation. The temptation takes place in the holy city of Jerusalem, on the 'little wing' of the temple. Jacob was reputed to be the most pious of men – praying constantly in the temple for his people.[129] His death was at the hands of others:

---

127 *The Septuagint Version of the Old Testament with an English translation and with various readings and critical notes* (London: Samuel Bagster and Sons, n.d.), 754.

128 Robert H. Gundry, *Matthew: A Commentary on His Handbook for a Mixed Church under Persecution*, 2nd ed. (Grand Rapids, Michigan: William B. Eerdmans, 1994), 57: "The Devil takes his quotation from Ps 91(90):11-12, but omits the phrase 'in all your ways' because the deliberate throwing of oneself from a high perch does not correspond to accidental stumbling over a stone on one's path (as in the psalm)."

129 From Hegesippus, in Eusebius, *Ecclesiastical History* (2.23), 171. "He alone was allowed to enter into the sanctuary, for he did not wear wool but linen, and he used to enter alone into the temple and be found kneeling and praying for forgiveness for the people, so that his knees grew hard like a camel's because of his constant worship of God, kneeling and asking forgiveness for the people. So from his excessive righteousness he was called the Just (*dikaios*) and Oblias (*oblias*), that is in Greek 'Rampart of the people and righteousness,' as the prophets declare concerning him."

he was made to stand on the edge of a high point of the temple, and was then (after speaking to the people below) thrown down onto the stone courtyard. He was stoned – that is, he suffered the capital punishment meted out to one who was found guilty of leading others astray. Finally, his head was bashed in with a wooden laundry club.

We are not yet very far into Matthew's narrative, yet because I believe Peter and Jacob are the foci of a 'Peter-Jacob' hidden story, it seems possible that the striking of one's foot against a stone is Matthew's allusion to a *skandalon* – a stumbling block. True, the word here is *lithos* (stone), rather than *petra* (rock), yet this is just one of the many features of this Gospel which incline us to see Matthew's mind at work; reflecting on the death of Jacob, and the part that Peter ('Rock') may have played in it.

The third temptation. Matthew 4:8-11

The third and final temptation sees the Devil offering Jesus the whole world, in return for Jesus' worship of the Devil.

> **Again, the devil (*diabolos*) took him to a very high mountain, and showed him all the kingdoms of the world and the glory of them; and he said to him, "All these I will give you, if you will fall down and worship me." Then Jesus said to him, "Begone, Satan (*hupage, satana*)! for it is written, 'You shall worship the Lord your God and him only shall you serve.'[130]" Then the devil left him, and behold, angels came and ministered to him. (Mt 4:8-11)**

For the first time in this Gospel we encounter the name 'Satan,'[131] when Jesus says to the devil, "Begone, Satan (*hupage, satana*)!" Those

---

130 Deut 6:13.
131 Davies and Allison, *Saint Matthew*, 1:372. "'Begone, Satan!' points to more than a verbal link with 16:21-3. In both places Jesus is choosing the path of duty: the end ordained by the Father is to be achieved by the manner ordained by the Father, namely, the cross. And any opposition to this is satanic. To reject the way of the cross is to be on the side of the devil."

who know this Gospel will recall that later Jesus says something very similar to Peter: "Get behind me, Satan (*hupage opisō mou, satana*)! You are a hindrance (*skandalon*) to me; for you are not on the side of God, but of men" (Mt 16:23). Peter has tried to stop Jesus from going to Jerusalem, with its inevitability of suffering and death.

Matthew's readers/hearers would most likely know the parallel in Mark 8:33: "But turning and seeing his disciples, he [Jesus] rebuked Peter, and said, 'Get behind me, Satan (*hupage opisō mou, satana*)! For you are not on the side of God, but of men.'" If Matthew is using Mark's Gospel as a basis for his own, then Matthew has added the words 'You are a *skandalon* to me,' which directly accuses Peter of being a *skandalon* – someone who causes others to trip up, or sin.

Conclusion

How credible is it that, in this narrative of the three temptations offered to Jesus in the desert, Matthew has inserted allusions to the death of Jacob, Jesus' brother – a death which occurred more than thirty years after Jesus' crucifixion? Yet there are several reasons to think that this is what Matthew is doing.

In the first temptation there is a reference to stones (Mt 4:3) – using the Greek word *lithoi* ('stones'), but not the Greek *petra/petros*, meaning 'rock.' We cannot say at this point that this is an allusion to Peter ('Rock').

The second temptation takes place in Jerusalem, where the devil sets Jesus on the little wing of the temple, and invites him to throw himself over the edge. The death of Jacob took place at this site, in 62 C.E., but he was thrown down by his adversaries rather than throwing himself off the 'little wing.' His body would have struck the stones (*lithoi*) below, injuring him greatly. His death was hastened by being stoned, and then by having his head beaten in.

In the third temptation scene Matthew has the words, "Begone, Satan (*hupage, satana*)!," which correspond closely to Jesus' later rebuke of Peter: "Get behind me, Satan (*hupage opisō mou, satana*)!," when Peter tries to deflect Jesus from journeying to Jerusalem and death. Jesus calls Peter a *skandalon*, "for you are not on the side of God, but of men" (Mt 16:21-23).

It would seem that Matthew has written this passage (Mt 4:4-11) in such a way that he has made allusions to the death of Jacob, and to Peter the *skandalon*.

— Chapter Six —

Jesus calls his first four disciples. Matthew 4:18-22

After his time in the desert Jesus goes first to Nazareth and then to Capernaum by the sea (Mt 4:13), where he begins to preach: "Repent, for the kingdom of heaven is at hand" (Mt 4:17). It is now, at the very beginning of his ministry, that Jesus calls four men – two from one family, and two from another – to be his disciples.

> **As he walked by the Sea of Galilee, he saw two brothers (*duo adelphous*), Simon who is called Peter (Petros) and Andrew his brother (*ton adelphon autou*), casting a net into the sea; for they were fishermen. And he said to them, "Follow me, and I will make you fishers of men." Immediately they left their nets and followed him. (Mt 4:18-20)**

It is "Simon who is called Peter" who is named first in this Gospel,[132] but no explanation is given for the name Peter (*Petros*, a

---

132 In John's Gospel, Simon Peter is not the first-called of the Twelve (Jn 1:40-42). That honour belongs to Andrew and the anonymous disciple, whom I have identified as Jesus' young brother Jacob. See Katherine C. Linforth, *The Beloved Disciple: Jacob the Brother of the Lord* (Fremantle, W.A: VIVID Publishing, 2014), 96.

masculine alternative to the Greek feminine *petra*, meaning 'rock'). Matthew's audience would certainly have known Peter by the name 'Rock,' rather than his given name Simon. It is not until well into Matthew's narrative that we find out what Simon's new name of 'Peter' implies (Mt 16:18). Even then, is it a re-naming of Simon as 'Peter,' or more a confirmation of identity?

From Robert H. Gundry[133]:

In 4:18-20 Matthew introduces Peter under the common personal name "Simon" (Greek for the Semitic "Symeon") and then adds "the one called Peter" (not in the par. Mark 1:16). This addition joins both the unusualness of "Peter" as a personal name, the mention of these two names ahead of "Andrew his brother," and the calling of Andrew "his brother" rather than vice versa ("Peter, the brother of Andrew") to make Peter prominent.

We note that Matthew uses the word 'brother'- "Andrew his brother"- although we have already been told that Peter and Andrew are brothers. This is also the case when Jesus encounters the next two men – James and John, the sons of Zebedee.

And going on from there he [Jesus] saw two other brothers (*allous duo adelphous*), James the son of Zebedee and John his brother (*adelphon autou*), in the boat with Zebedee their father, mending their nets, and he called them. Immediately they left the boat and their father, and followed him. (Mt 4:21-22)

These fishermen are the only people in Matthew's Gospel (apart from the tax-collector in Matthew 9:9) who receive a personal call from Jesus to follow him.

Why this emphasis on 'brothers/brother'? Robert Gundry and

---

[133] Robert H. Gundry, *Peter: False Disciple and Apostate according to Saint Matthew* (Grand Rapids, Michigan/Cambridge, U.K.: William B. Eerdmans, 2015), 6.

other scholars see it as reflecting Matthew's ideal of church community; the brotherhood of believers.[134]

Certainly, throughout his Gospel Matthew is deeply concerned with the 'brotherhood' of the Christian community, but the theme of biological brotherhood is also very important to him. I believe that the reason lies in the biological brotherhood of Jesus and his younger brother Jacob. Matthew is entering on a theme (the 'Jacob and Peter' story) which is an undercurrent to the primary, overt story of Jesus.

Conclusion

My lecturer in Matthew's Gospel, the late Brother Rod Doyle cfc[135], raised this point when discussing Matthew 4:18-22. Why did Matthew repeat 'brothers' and 'brother'? Rod's conclusion was that the stress on 'brother/s' throughout the Gospel reflected Matthew's earnest wish for the community of Christians to live together in a state of brotherhood. However, the query about the repetition of 'brother/s' stayed with me, and this work is the result – the story of Jacob the brother of Jesus, and of Peter.

---

134 Robert H. Gundry, *Matthew: A Commentary on His Handbook for a Mixed Church under Persecution*, 2nd ed. (Grand Rapids, Michigan: William B. Eerdmans, 1994), 62. "This overuse of $αδελφος$ carries on the theme of churchly brotherhood, symbolized by the family relationship of James and John."

135 Lecturer in Biblical Studies and Biblical Greek, Catholic Theological College, Melbourne, Australia.

– Chapter Seven –

Anger against a brother. Matthew 5:21-26

Jesus is speaking:
> You have heard that it was said to the men of old, 'You shall not kill; and whoever kills shall be liable to judgment.' But I say to you that every one who is angry (*ho orgizomenos*) with his brother shall be liable to judgment; whoever insults his brother [says to his brother, '*raka*'] shall be liable to the council (*sunedriō*), and whoever says, 'You fool (*mōre*)!' shall be liable to the hell of fire. (Mt 5:21-22)

> So if you are offering your gift at the altar, and there remember that your brother has something against you, leave your gift there before the altar and go (*hupage*); first (*prōton*) be reconciled to your brother, and then come and offer your gift. (Mt 5:23-24)

> Make friends quickly with your accuser, while you are going with him (*met autou en tē hōdo*; lit., 'with him

on/in the way'[136]) **lest your accuser hand you over to the judge, and the judge to the guard, and you be put in prison; truly, I say to you, you will never get out till you have paid the last penny. (Mt 5:25-26).**

The passage falls naturally into three sections: vv. 21-22, 23-24, and 25-26. The passage is part of the great Sermon on the Mount and follows on from Jesus speaking of the law and the prophets, which he has come to fulfil, not to abolish (Mt 5:17). "Whoever then relaxes one of the least of these commandments and teaches men so, shall be called least in the kingdom of heaven; but he who does them and teaches them shall be called great in the kingdom of heaven" (Mt 5:19).

Matthew 5:21-22

Jesus reminds his hearers of the commandment not to kill (Ex 20:13; Deut 5:17): the consequence of this, according to Matthew 5:21, is judgement (*tē krisei* = 'the judgement'). Unexpectedly, Jesus goes on to say that the one who is angry (*ho orgizomenos*) with his brother is equally liable to judgement (*tē krisei*). This seems almost to equate anger against a brother with murdering that brother. (A similar idea is expressed in the letter referred to as the first letter of John, but which I believe is a letter of Jacob, Jesus' brother.[137] "Anyone who hates his brother is a murderer, and you know that no murderer has eternal life abiding in him"(1 Jn 3:15).)

"Whoever is angry with" is the usual translation of *orgizomenos* (the root of our English word 'orgy'), the first of the three crimes listed in our verse. "Anger" is a temporary "orgy," a fit of madness. (In English we even speak

---

136 RSV adds 'to court.'
137 Katherine C. Linforth, T*he Beloved Disciple: Jacob the Brother of the Lord* (Fremantle, W.A.: VIVID Publishing, 2014), 211-235.

of "getting mad" or "being mad"; the Stoics called anger *brevem insaniam*, "a brief insanity" ... However, the grammatical construction here is more extensive than the usual translation "is angry"; *orgizomenos* is a present-tense *participle* and so literally means "is *being* angry," "is *carrying* anger," "is *remaining* angry," or the nicely descriptive idiom, "is *nursing a grudge*."[138] [Bruner's emphases]

Bruner concludes that 'resenting' - an ongoing anger - might be the best translation.[139]

So it seems like a situation of ongoing resentment is being described, not a one-off flare-up of anger. For me, this could possibly describe a continuing resentment on Peter's part towards Jacob. Jacob had taken over leadership of the Christian Jewish communities (not just in Jerusalem but in the diaspora) when Peter was forced, in fear of his own life, to leave Jerusalem (Acts 12:17). This was in the early forties, and from that time onward Jacob was the one to whom all matters would be directed, and whose authority would be paramount.

Peter had most probably 'mentored' Jacob as Jacob was growing up, but from the early forties it was Jacob who had authority even over Peter. Peter was obviously back in Jerusalem earlier, for the Council of Jerusalem (Acts 15:4-11). Was he back in Jerusalem again in 62 C.E., for the Passover festival? Did he and Jacob have a heated exchange of words, in which insults were exchanged? Did Peter then say something derogatory about Jacob to someone who then told the Scribes and Pharisees? Was Jacob put in a bad light: instead of being Jacob the Righteous could he now be accused of having acted 'unrighteously'? This would have given Jacob's enemies their excuse to get rid of him.

---

138 Frederick Dale Bruner, *Matthew: a commentary*, Rev. ed. (Grand Rapids, Michigan/Cambridge, U.K.: William B. Eerdmans, 2004), 208.
139 Bruner, *Matthew*, 209.

With the talk of 'brothers' (Mt 5:21-22) – which can mean biological brothers, as well as brothers in the Christian community – many commentators at this point pick up the allusion to the killing of Abel by his brother Cain (Gen 4:8). As R.T. France says:

> The wording of this pericope may carry a deliberate echo of the story of Cain (alluded to also in Matt 18:22 and 23:25), who, because he was angry (Gen 4:5-6), murdered his brother (Gen 4:8), the problem having arisen from their respective offerings (Gen 4:3-5); cf. here v. 23); but, if so, the parallel is not exploited.[140]

For those readers/listeners of Matthew's time who were aware of the circumstances of Jacob's death, there would have been no need for the parallel to be exploited. This Matthean episode (Mt 5:21-26) is giving us the likely background; Peter's resentment of Jacob; an occasion when Peter and Jacob were angry with each other, and exchanged insults. The possibility of a reconciliation between them simply didn't happen; all this at a time when one of the protagonists was bringing a sacrificial gift to the altar in the Jerusalem temple, at the festival of Passover.

Matthew outlines the consequences of this anger and insulting language: both parties will be liable to judgement. The one who calls his brother '*raka!*' will be liable to the Sanhedrin (the Jerusalem council), and the one who calls his brother '*mōre* ('fool')' will be liable to the fire of Gehenna (Mt 5:22). According to Davies and Allison, *raka* is a "contemptuous insult: 'empty-headed', 'good for nothing', 'fool'."[141] As regards *mōre*: "usually translated, 'you fool' ... Some, however, have equated it with the Hebrew *moreh* (= 'rebel'; cf.

---

140 R.T. France, *The Gospel of Matthew* (Grand Rapids, Michigan/Cambridge, U.K.: William B. Eerdmans, 2007), 199. Footnote 76.

141 W.D. Davies and Dale C. Allison, *A Critical and Exegetical Commentary on the Gospel according to Saint Matthew*, Vol. 1, Matthew I-VII (London/New York: T&T Clark, 2004), 513.

Deut 21:18, 20..."[142]

If I am right, and it is Peter and Jacob about whom Matthew is writing, who used these particular insults? Was it Jacob who called Peter '*raka*', for which offence one was then liable to be called up by the Sanhedrin? Was it Peter who called Jacob '*mōre*' (in the sense of 'rebel'), and who used that word in relation to Jacob when he (Peter) was speaking to others? I don't see Jacob as blameless in the altercation, but many indications in Matthew's Gospel lead me to think that it was Peter who was in danger of hellfire (Gehenna), for calling Jacob '*mōre*'. The punishment of 'hellfire' can only suggest that Matthew believed that Peter spoke openly against Jacob, calling him a 'rebel' (against the Law). The suggestion would have been taken up by the Jerusalem hierarchy, which would have welcomed an opportunity to have Jacob publicly disgraced, and executed.

Something that adds weight to Jacob being the one to call Peter '*raka*' is the particular consequence – being brought before the Sanhedrin (Mt 5:22). In Josephus's account of Jacob's 'trial' and death, he says: "And so he [the high priest Ananus] convened the judges of the Sanhedrin and brought before them a man named James [Jacob], the brother of Jesus who was called the Christ, and certain others."[143]

Matthew 5:23-24

The allusion to the Cain and Abel story is even more pronounced in the next passage, with the offering of a gift before the altar. Jesus gives an illustration concerning two brothers: one brings his gift to the altar in the temple, but Jesus says the gift must be left before the altar until the gift-bearer finds his brother and effects a reconciliation with him. Only then can the gift be offered at the altar.

---

142 Davies and Allison, *Saint Matthew*, 1:514.
143 Josephus, *Jewish Antiquities*, Books XVIII-XX, Louis H. Feldman, trans., Loeb Classical Library (London: William Heinemann/Cambridge, Mass.: Harvard University Press, 1965), 495, 497.

There is a noticeable change of pronouns in these verses: 'you' is no longer plural (as in verses 21-22) but second person singular. It is now an individual who is being addressed.

So if you are offering your gift at the altar, and there remember that your brother has something against you, leave your gift there before the altar and go (*hupage*); first (*prōton*) be reconciled to your brother, and then come and offer your gift.

Something that should make us reflect is the fact that speaking of 'gifts' and 'altar' would be anachronistic to Matthew's readers/hearers, in the late sixties or seventies.

If the verse has to do with fellow believers in a Christian community (cf. 18:15-20), as it must if 'brother' means 'Christian brother', it is a bit awkward for the evangelist to go on to mention the sanhedrin (5:22), the altar (5:23-4), and the prison (5:25-6): these are not peculiarly Christian things.[144]

The Sanhedrin, the altar, the temple and the priesthood were certainly not relevant post-70 C.E., after the siege of Jerusalem by the Roman army, and the destruction of the temple. If, as I believe, Matthew 5:23-24 is describing a heated exchange between Peter and Jacob, what would the argument have been about? Is there a clue in some previous words ascribed to Jesus?

Jesus has said:

Whoever then relaxes one of the least of these commandments and teaches men so, shall be called least in the kingdom of heaven; but he who does them and teaches them shall be called great in the kingdom of heaven. (Mt 5:19)

If Peter was in Jerusalem for Passover in 62 C.E., did Jacob call him to account for 'relaxing' the commandments in the Christian

---

144 Davies and Allison, *Saint Matthew*, 1:512-513.

communities outside Jerusalem? Peter had certainly been in Antioch, probably in Corinth and Rome, and possibly in other parts of the Mediterranean for many years. Had Peter's everyday contact with Gentiles led him to 'relaxing' (at least in Jacob's eyes) the Law? Did Peter resent the younger man, Jacob, because of his position of authority and his reputation for 'righteousness'? Were insults exchanged? Did Peter then say something to one of the scribes, Pharisees, or high-priestly clan which gave them a lever to get rid of Jacob?

From Donald A. Hagner:

In our context, the statement 'your brother has something against you' must be taken to imply some degree of anger in the person offering the sacrifice. (We would expect 'you have something against your brother,' as in Mark 11:25.[145])
Perhaps we are to understand a reciprocal resentment.[146]

If Matthew has used Mark's Gospel as a basis for his, then he has changed the situation of the quarrelling brothers. It is the one offering the gift - the one who feels wronged, the one nursing an ongoing resentment - who needs to initiate a reconciliation with his brother.

First (*prōton*); Go (*hupage*)

Matthew, in a characteristic 'sandwich' device, highlights something significant by enclosing it between two other sentences containing the same word/idea. In Matthew 5:23-24 there are three instances of the word 'gift.' Between the first two instances of 'gift' is the message about remembering that your brother "has something against you." Then between the second 'gift' and the third 'gift' is the phrase "go;

---

145 Mk 11:25. "And whenever you stand praying, forgive, if you have anything against any one; so that your Father also who is in heaven may forgive you your trespasses."

146 Donald A. Hagner, *Matthew 1-13* (Dallas, Texas: Word Books, c.1993), 117.

first ...": "leave your gift there before the altar and go (*hupage*); first (*prōton*) be reconciled to your brother ..." The juxtaposition of 'go' and 'first' has a clumsy feel to it, which leaves scholars attempting elucidation.

From Davies and Allison: "πρωτον could connect up with the earlier imperative, 'go'; but the sense demands that we read, 'first be reconciled... *then* coming offer your gift.'"[147] [Davies' and Allison's emphases]

But Matthew writes what he writes because he has a hidden story to tell. He is writing 'first' and 'go' to make the association with Peter. This is Matthew indicating, as pointedly as he can, that it is Peter who is the angry temple-visitor and gift-bringer. Peter is the only disciple in this Gospel to be called 'first' (Mt 10:2: *prōtos Simon*),[148] and the only disciple to whom Jesus says 'Go!': "But he [Jesus] turned and said to Peter, 'Get behind me, Satan! (*hupage opisō mou, satana*); for you are not on the side of God but of men" (Mt 16:23). Surely we are meant to bring this association to mind, when reading/hearing Matthew 5:23-24.

Matthew 5:25-26

Make friends quickly with your accuser, while you are going with him (*en tē hodō* = 'on/in the way'),[149] lest your accuser hand you over to the judge, and the judge to the guard, and you be put in prison; truly I say to you, you will never get out till you have paid the last penny.

These two men are 'on the way (*en tē hodō*)' together, which

---

147 Davies and Allison, *Saint Matthew*, 1:518.

148 Hagner, *Matthew 1-13*, 265-6. Re Mt 10:2: "The πρῶτος before 'Simon, who is called Peter' implies not just the first called but the first in rank (cf. 16:18). Peter plays a most prominent role in the Gospel as the spokesman for the apostles but most importantly as the rock (hence, 'Peter') upon which Jesus promises to build his Church ... "

149 RSV adds 'to court.'

implies more than it says at first reading. The very early Jesus-followers were known as people of 'the Way' – that is, the Way of Jesus (Acts 9:2; 18:25; 19:9, 23; 22:4; 24:14, 22). Here Matthew is referring to two men who are both followers of 'the Way' – the Way of Jesus.[150] They are then 'brothers' in the Matthean sense of being members of the community, but each also has a biological brother; Andrew is Peter's brother and Jesus is Jacob's brother.

Is the accuser (*antidikos*) Jacob? Has he accused Peter of 'relaxing' the Jewish Law, in the communities outside Jerusalem? Has he insulted Peter by calling him '*raka* (fool)!'? And has Peter then responded by calling Jacob '*mōre* (fool/rebel against God),' and then using that word (in the sense of 'rebel against the Law') to the Scribes and Pharisees in regard to Jacob?

Is the judge in these two verses God himself, who will judge at the end of the age? If the gift-bringer doesn't seek reconciliation with his brother, he will be handed over to the judge, then to the guard, and finally will be imprisoned until the last penny has been paid. This sounds odd, because until now no monetary debt has been mentioned.

There is a link between the story of the two brothers at loggerheads in Matthew 5:21-26 and the story of the two debtors in Matthew 18:23-25. The resentful 'brother' in Matthew 5:25-26 is warned that he will be imprisoned, and will never get out till he has paid the last penny. One of the servants, in Matthew 18:23-25, who has shown no \mercy to a fellow servant, finds himself "delivered him to the jailers, till he should pay all his debt" (Mt 18:34).

This story of the two servants follows Peter's (highly personal) question to Jesus about how many times he (Peter) should forgive a brother who wrongs him (Mt 18:21-22). Peter suggests seven times

---

150 Luke Timothy Johnson, *The Acts of the Apostles* (Collegeville, Minnesota: The Liturgical Press, 1992), 162.

(which sounds quite generous), but Jesus responds with 'seventy-seven times,' meaning Peter's forgiveness of his 'brother' should be unlimited.

It is important to know the meaning of the Greek verb *aphiēmi*, which is usually translated as 'forgive.' The sense of the verb *aphiēmi* is 'leave,' 'let alone,' leave behind.' We English-speakers of the twenty-first century tend to think that forgiveness is almost saying "what happened doesn't matter," "the offender need not be held to account," etc. Yet this sort of 'forgiveness' is impossible when there has been grievous harm committed, particularly to someone we love and respect. We cannot say that it doesn't matter, or that the offender should not be held accountable for his/her act.

I believe that Matthew is saying that the offended person has to 'let go' of anger and thoughts of vengeance, because the only judgement is judgement by God. ("Judge not, that you be not judged. For with the judgment you pronounce you will be judged, and the measure you give will be the measure you get." Mt 7:1-2.)

Because this story of the debtors is, I believe, alluding to Peter and Jacob, it is given here in full.

Matthew 18:23-35

Therefore the kingdom of heaven may be compared to a king who wished to settle accounts with his servants. When he began the reckoning, one was brought to him who owed him ten thousand talents; and as he could not pay, his lord ordered him to be sold, with his wife and children and all that he had, and payment to be made. So the servant fell on his knees, imploring him, "Lord, have patience with me, and I will pay you everything." And out of pity for him the lord of that servant released him and forgave him the debt. But that same servant, as he went out, came upon one of his fellow servants who owed him a hundred denarii; and seizing him by the throat he said, "Pay what you owe."

So his fellow servant fell down and besought him, "Have patience with me, and I will pay you." He refused and went and put him in prison till he should pay the debt. When his fellow servants saw what had taken place, they were greatly distressed, and they went and reported to their lord all that had taken place. Then his lord summoned him and said to him, "You wicked servant! I forgave you all that debt because you besought me; and should not you have had mercy on your fellow servant, as I had mercy on you?" And in anger his lord delivered him to the jailers (*basanistais* = 'torturers') till he should pay all his debt. So also my heavenly Father will do to every one of you, if you do not forgive your brother from your heart.

Where else in this Gospel do we hear about forgiving one's debtors? It is part of the prayer to 'Our Father' that Jesus teaches his disciples: "And forgive us our debts, as we also have forgiven our debtors" (Mt 6:12). As God has mercy on us and forgives us our sins, so we also must be merciful, and forgive our 'brothers' their sins against us.

What does this story of the two debtors say, in the context of the Peter-Jacob story'? The king represents God, and perhaps the setting is the judgement at the end of the age. I believe that the first servant brought before the king represents Peter, who owes a huge 'debt' to God for his (Peter's) denials of Jesus. On the night when Jesus was taken to the high priest's residence, Peter stood in the courtyard and three times denied knowing Jesus, while swearing and cursing (Mt 26:69-75). This is a huge 'debt' to be forgiven, and from which to be released.

In the story the king is filled with tenderness towards the servant, who has pleaded for patience with him, and for time to repay the debt (Mt 18:26-27). The king forgives the servant his debt, and sets him free (Mt 18:27). But it is the behaviour of this first servant against a fellow servant which is at the heart of this story. The first servant refuses to forgive the fellow servant who owes him a small amount, or to give him time to repay the debt: he treats him with violence, and has him put in prison.

I believe this second servant is Jacob, whom Peter is unable to forgive for offending him. Events gather momentum, after Peter says something adverse about Jacob to someone else who wants to see Jacob brought down.

Chapter Eight

First, Simon. Matthew 10:1-2

Matthew 10:1-4 is a brief narrative concerning Jesus' calling to himself twelve of his followers, to become Jesus' inner group of disciples. Matthew names them all[151]; but the first four names are the ones of interest in the context of the Peter-Jacob story.

> **And he [Jesus] called to him his twelve disciples and gave them authority over unclean spirits, to cast them out, and to heal every disease and infirmity. The names of the twelve apostles are these: first (*prōtos*), Simon, who is called Peter (*Petros*),[152] and Andrew his brother; James the son of Zebedee, and John his brother. (Mt 10:1-2)**

The first four names are a repetition of the first four names in Matthew 4:18, 21; "Simon who is called Peter and Andrew his brother..." and "James the son of Zebedee and John his brother ...",

---

151 Cf. Mk 3:16-19; Lk 6:13-16.
152 R.T. France, *The Gospel of Matthew* (Grand Rapids, Michigan/Carlisle, U.K.: William B. Eerdmans, 2007), 378. "By Matthew's time the first apostle was generally known as 'Peter' rather than 'Simon,' and so Matthew uses 'Peter' even before that name is formally given in the narrative sequence at 16:18: his narrative uses 'Simon' (always in connection with 'Peter') only when he being introduced, here and in 4:18, and on the occasion of his renaming in 16:16-17."

except for the inclusion of the word 'first (*prōtos*).' Simon Peter is first-named in the list of the Twelve, but 'first' has a further implication.

The πρωτος before 'Simon, who is called Peter' implies not just the first called but the first in rank (cf. 16:18). Peter plays a most prominent role in the Gospel as the spokesman for the apostles but most importantly as the rock (hence, 'Peter') upon which Jesus promises to build his Church (twenty-three occurrences; see esp. 14:28-29; 16:16-19; 18:21; 19:27; 26:33-35).[153]

First (*prōtos*)

Peter may have been considered first in rank in the three Synoptic Gospels, but the fact that Matthew calls Peter 'first (*prōtos*)' is significant in relation to this present work. There are at least four particular passages in this Gospel where the word 'first (*prōtos*)' is used, that may allude to Peter. These are Matthew 5:24 (explored in the previous chapter of this work); 19:30; 20:16; and 20:26-27.

In Matthew 19:27, Peter says to Jesus, "Lo, we have left everything and followed you. What then shall we have?" Jesus assures his Twelve that they will sit on the twelve thrones in the "new world," and those who have left everything in this life to follow him will receive "a hundredfold, and inherit eternal life." However Jesus ends with: "But many that are first (*prōtoi*) will be last (*eschatoi*), and the last (*eschatoi*) first (*prōtoi*)" (Mt 19:30). Is this possibly a warning to Peter (the 'first' of the Twelve) of the cost of discipleship? Perhaps Peter is counting up what he might lose in material terms, by following Jesus.

Another instance of 'first,' which may be significant in terms of Peter, is at the end of the parable of the householder who hires labourers to work in his vineyard (Mt 20:1-16). The householder

---

153 Donald A. Hagner, *Matthew 1-13* (Dallas, Texas: Word Books, c1993), 265-6.

promises a certain wage to the first labourers who are hired, but at the end of the day even those labourers hired late in the day are given the same wage. There are complaints from those hired early in the day that the late-comers are being given the same wage as they receive. The householder reminds the first-hired labourers of their original agreement, and says: "So the last (*eschatoi*) will be first (*prōtoi*) and the first (*prōtoi*) last (*eschatoi*)" (Mt 20:16). Is it Peter (the 'first' to follow Jesus) who is upset by what he sees as a lack of fairness, in regard to himself and later disciples of Jesus?

This parable is shortly followed by the narrative concerning the mother of James and John of Zebedee, who brings her sons to Jesus and asks that they be the ones to sit at Jesus' right and left hand in the kingdom (Mt 20:20-21). This causes indignation among the rest of the Twelve, leading Jesus to gives a lesson about 'greatness': "... whoever would be great among you must be your servant, and whoever would be first (*prōtos*) among you must be your slave" (Mt 20:26-27). Is this a reminder to Peter, the 'first' of the Twelve, that true greatness is in being a servant to others?

For consideration

Matthew's Gospel is the only one of the Synoptic Gospels in which the word 'first (*prōtos*)' is closely associated with Simon Peter (Mt 10:2). While not all occurrences of *prōtos* in the Gospel refer to Peter, we need to keep in mind the possibility that some of them do.

Matthew 10:2 speaks of the Twelve as 'apostles'; that is, after Jesus' crucifixion they are to go out into the world to proclaim the Gospel. This is made explicit in Matthew 28:19, when Jesus tells his eleven disciples: "Go therefore and make disciples of all nations, baptizing them in the name of the Father and of the Son and of the Holy Spirit." Matthew is, I believe, not only telling a story about Jesus in c 30 C.E.; he is also telling a story about Peter and Jacob, thirty years after Jesus' crucifixion.

Chapter Nine

A sparrow falls to the ground. Matthew 10:24-33

A disciple is not above his teacher, nor a servant above his master; it is enough for the disciple to be like his teacher, and the servant like his master. (Mt 10:24-25a)

If they have called the master of the house Be-elzebul, how much more will they malign those of his household. (Mt 10:25b)

So have no fear of them; for nothing is covered that will not be revealed, or hidden that will not be known. What I tell you in the dark, utter in the light; and what you hear whispered, proclaim upon the housetops. (Mt 10:26-27)

And do not fear those who kill the body but cannot kill the soul; rather fear him who can destroy both soul and body in hell. (Mt 10:28)

Are not two sparrows sold for a penny? And not one of them will fall to the ground without your Father.[154] But

---

154 RSV has "without your Father's will."

> even the hairs of your head are all numbered. Fear not, therefore; you are of more value than many sparrows. (Mt 10:29-31)
>
> So every one who acknowledges me before men, I also will acknowledge before my Father who is in heaven; but whoever denies me before men, I also will deny before my Father who is in heaven. (Mt 10:32-33)

I have intentionally arranged Matthew 10:24-33 in the format above, to show more clearly Jesus' teachings to the twelve chosen disciples, now to be apostles (Mt 10:2,5). The passage contains:

    a. A warning against self-aggrandisement (believing oneself greater than one's teacher or master) (vv. 24-25a).

    b. A warning that those opposed to the 'master of the house' (Jesus) will also be opposed to the master's followers (v. 25b).

    c. The promise of a revelation at some future point – something now covered will be revealed; something now hidden will become known (v. 26). What is told in the dark will be spoken about in the light; what is whispered now will be shouted from the rooftops (v. 27).

    d. A warning about the one (God?) who can bring about the destruction of both body and soul in hell (v. 28).

    e. A reference to two little birds (*strouthia*) sold for a penny, and not one of them falling to the ground "without your Father" (v. 29). This is followed by the assurance to Jesus' disciples that "'even the hairs of your head are all numbered "(v. 30). A further assurance follows, that "you are of more value than many sparrows" (v. 31).

    f. A final warning – that anyone who denies Jesus in this life ("before men") will find Jesus denying him/her before his Father in heaven (v. 32).

What are we to make of this assortment of rather obscure sayings of Jesus? I propose that these sayings are primarily Matthean – that is, the Evangelist, writing some thirty years after Jesus' crucifixion, has put into the mouth of Jesus sayings which apply not only generally, but more specifically to Peter and Jacob, at the time when Jacob was put to death in Jerusalem. Let us look closely at these sayings, with regard to a Peter-Jacob context.

Matthew 10:24-25
A disciple is not above his teacher, nor a servant above his master; it is enough for the disciple to be like his teacher, and the servant like his master.[155]

If Matthew is alluding to Peter and Jacob, as I believe he is doing, then who is the disciple who is not above his teacher, and who is the servant (*doulos* = 'slave') who is not above his master/lord? Both Peter and Jacob could be said to be disciples of Jesus, although Jacob was not one of the Twelve. How did each refer to himself, in the years after the crucifixion of Jesus? Jacob, in his letter to the churches of the diaspora, calls himself "a servant (*doulos*)[156] of God and of the Lord Jesus Christ" (Jas 1:1). He calls himself a *doulos*, not an apostle, or even a disciple.

Peter, in a letter attributed to him, introduces himself as "Peter, an apostle (*apostolos*) of Jesus Christ" (1 Pet 1:1), while another Petrine letter begins: "Peter, a servant (*doulos*) and apostle (*apostolos*) of Jesus Christ ..." (2 Pet 1:1). The Petrine letters omit the word

---

155 W.D. Davies and Dale C. Allison, *A Critical and Exegetical Commentary on the Gospel according to Saint Matthew*, Vol. 2, Matthew VIII-XVIII (London/New York: T&T Clark, 2004), 194. "Although never the teacher's equal, the disciple can aspire to be like the teacher, and the servant can aspire to be like the Lord. The theme is the imitation of Christ: Christians must follow Christ's example."

156 R.T. France, *The Gospel of Matthew* (Grand Rapids, Michigan/Cambridge, U.K.: William B. Eerdmans, 2007), 401: "[But] for Jesus during his ministry to speak of his own disciples as his douloi, 'slaves,' is an extension of the metaphor which is unique in this gospel, though the apostolic writers were of course happy to describe themselves as douloi of the risen Christ (Rom 1:1; Gal 1:10; Phil 1:1 etc; Jas 1:1; 2 Peter 1:1; Jude 1:1).".

'Lord,' saying simply 'Jesus Christ.' There is scholarly contention about the authenticity of both Petrine letters, particularly in regard to 2 Peter.

Is Matthew warning Peter (the 'disciple') not to see himself above Jesus, his teacher? And Is Matthew also warning Jacob (the 'servant') not to think of himself as being above his master, Jesus? Both Peter and Jacob were the leaders in their own territories – Jacob in Jerusalem, as well as the Christian Jewish communities of the diaspora, and Peter in the Christian communities of cosmopolitan Rome. Is Matthew giving a warning that such positions hold the danger of growing self-importance, of forgetting the message of Jesus that he who wants to become great must become both servant and slave (Mt 20:26-27)?

Matthew 10:26-27

So have no fear of them; for nothing is covered that will not be revealed, or hidden that will not be known. What I tell you in the dark, utter in the light; and what you hear whispered, proclaim upon the housetops. (Mt 10:26-27)

What is the secret knowledge that will one day be revealed, even shouted out publicly? The meaning of this passage is difficult, and commentators struggle to find a suitable interpretation. From France:

> [But] v. 27 is about the disciples' duty to proclaim their message openly, and that proclamation would be the first casualty of a fear inspired by their opponents. The disciples' duty is not merely the negative one of avoiding fear, but the positive one of bold proclamation in the face of opposition.[157]

And from Davies and Allison: "... on the last day God will see to it that the truth will be victorious."[158] Further, "although that which is

---

157 France, *Matthew*, 402.
158 Davies and Allison, *Saint Matthew*, 2:203.

hidden will be revealed (v. 26), this is something the disciples should not simply wait for or expect. They themselves are called to bring it about proleptically, that is, to make known the truth and those who belong to it."[159]

These are standard responses to these verses, which can be seen as part of Matthew's theme of true discipleship. But what if Matthew is also speaking of something quite specific? What if he is speaking of the execution of Jacob, and the circumstances which led to his death; that event which happened some thirty years after Jesus' crucifixion, and so is not part of Matthew's 'Jesus story'? Is Matthew saying, in 10:26-27, that at some time in the future this story would become known, while in Matthew's own time it was hidden, in order to save the young churches from confusion and doubt?

A scandal such as this – Simon Peter, the 'first' of the Twelve, implicated in the death of Jesus' brother Jacob - would have rocked the young church communities, and perhaps led to their disappearance. Yet, in Matthew's eyes, the matter was so grave, so heinous, that it had to be recorded somewhere, somehow, for a future generation.

With the words "proclaim upon the housetops," we recall Hegesippus's account of Jacob's death. Jacob is made to stand on the little wing of the temple (the 'house' of God) and is told proclaim against Jesus as the Messiah, to the Passover crowd below. Instead, Jacob makes a loud and final confession of faith: "Why do you ask me concerning the Son of Man? He is sitting in heaven on the right hand of the great power, and he will come on the clouds of heaven."[160] Is this the proclamation that Matthew has in mind; Jacob's very public confession of faith in Jesus Messiah?

---

159 Davies and Allison, *Saint Matthew*, 2:204.
160 Hegesippus, in Eusebius, *The Ecclesiastical History*, Books I-V, Kirsopp Lake, trans., Loeb Classical Library (Cambridge, Mass./London: Harvard University Press, 1926), 173.

Matthew 10:28

And do not fear those who kill the body but cannot kill the soul; rather fear him who can destroy both soul and body in hell. (Mt 10:28)

Persecution then, to the point of death, is not to be feared, if one is a true disciple of Jesus; but the destruction of both body and soul is the fate of those who align themselves against Jesus and his Father in heaven. Jacob has been killed because of the actions of others, but he is not separated from God the Father. It is Peter, I believe Matthew to be saying, who, by giving Jacob's opponents a means to entrap him, is in terrible danger of hell-fire. Has Matthew picked up this saying from Jacob's letter: "There is one lawgiver and judge, he who is able to save and to destroy" (Jas 4:12)?[161]

My readers, having come this far, may say that my theory is far-fetched, but the following two verses give weight to my argument that it is the death of Jacob, and Peter's culpability in that, which Matthew has in his mind.

Matthew 10:29-31

Are not two sparrows (*strouthia*) sold for a penny? And not one of them will fall to the ground without your Father. [162] But even the hairs of your head are all numbered.[163] Fear not, therefore; you are of more value than many sparrows (*strouthiōn*). (Mt 10:29-31)

---

161 Robert H. Gundry, Matthew: *A Commentary on His Handbook for a Mixed Church undergoing Persecution*, 2nd ed. (Grand Rapids, Michigan: Williams B. Eerdmans, 1994), 197. "See Jas 4:12 against identifying the one to fear as the Devil."

162 RSV has "without your Father's will."

163 Donald A. Hagner, *Matthew 1-13* (Dallas, Texas: Word Books, c1993), 286. "The numbering of the hairs on a head is a variant of the more common idea that when God protects, not even a single hair of a person's head is allowed to perish (e.g., 1 Sam 14:45; 2 Sam 14:11; Luke 21:18, Acts 27:34."

Here we have four sentences, and in each of the first and the last sentences there is a reference to sparrows (*strouthia*). From Leon Morris: "στρουθιον is a diminutive of στρουθος, 'sparrow,' and thus means 'little sparrow'; Jesus cites a very small bird and uses a diminutive even of that!"[164] These tiny birds are so small that one could buy two of them for one 'penny.' I believe that this diminutive 'sparrow' is Matthew's referencing of Jacob, whose nickname from childhood was '*Mikros*' (meaning 'small' or 'little').[165]

This passage is a Matthean 'sandwich,' whereby the most important message is contained within the two outer sentences with their references to sparrows. The middle sentences read:

And not one of them will fall to the ground without your Father. But even the hairs of your head are all numbered. (Mt 10:29b-30)

I believe these two sentences allude to the death of Jacob ('*Mikros*' – the little one), who fell to ground when he was thrown from the little wing of the temple in Jerusalem. Matthew is saying that Jacob, in his fall, was not abandoned by the Father (Mt 10:29b).[166] From Hegesippus we know that the fatal blow was delivered by a man wielding a wooden laundry-club, beating Jacob's head in.[167] (Jacob's hair may have been a distinctive feature of his physical appearance; according to Hegesippus, "no razor went upon his head."[168]) Matthew tells us that "even the hairs of your head are all numbered" (Mt 10:30). Jacob is still in God's care, even at the moment of his death.

---

164 Leon Morris, *The Gospel according to Matthew* (Grand Rapids, Michigan: William B. Eerdmans/Leicester, England: Inter-Varsity Press, 1992), 263. Footnote 66.

165 Linforth, Katherine, *The Beloved Disciple: Jacob the Brother of the Lord* (Fremantle, W.A.: VIVID Publishing, 2014), 26-33.

166 Davies and Allison, *Saint Matthew*, 2:207. "God is sovereign, so whatever happens must, despite appearances, somehow be within his will."

167 Hegesippus, in Eusebius, *Ecclesiastical History* (2.23), 175.

168 Hegesippus, in Eusebius, *Ecclesiastical History* (2.23), 171.

At this point we might recall the hint that Matthew has given us in the genealogy, where 'Amos' is listed (Mt 1:10). No Amos is to be found in the genealogies in Kings and Chronicles, but here in Matthew 10:29 Matthew would have us recall the words of the prophet Amos:

Will a bird fall on the earth without a fowler? (LXX: Amos 3:59).

This 'Amos' reference re-inforces the suggestion that Matthew is alluding to Jacob's death. The bird in Amos 3:5 is brought to the ground (and to its death) by a fowler. I believe that, throughout this Gospel, Matthew will give us reason to believe that Peter was the 'fowler' who set in motion the actions that led to Jacob's death.

Matthew 10:32-33

So every one who acknowledges me before men, I also will acknowledge before my Father who is in heaven; but whoever denies me before men, I also will deny before my Father who is in heaven. (Mt 10:32-33)

These are the words of Jesus, speaking to the Twelve before he sends them out (Mt 10:5). The teachings of Mathew 10:5-15 would seem to be applicable to that period of history – that is, before Jesus' death and resurrection. But the following counsels (Mt 10:16-42) would seem to describe events later than the crucifixion; persecution, testifying before governors, kings and Gentiles; and betrayal within families. Jesus' solemn pronouncement warns all his followers:

He who finds his life will lose it, and he who loses his life for my sake will find it. (Mt 10:39)

Matthew 10:32-33 is part of what I see as this post-resurrection narrative, and it calls on Jesus' followers to 'confess (*homologeō*[169])' him in public; that is, to make public their belief that Jesus is the

---

169 Vb *homologeō*. 'confess,' 'declare,' 'acknowledge,' 'profess.'

son of the Father, and to declare their allegiance to Jesus as Lord, as Jacob did. We know that Jacob 'confessed' Jesus publicly, but, in the context of Matthew 10:32-33, what do we make of Peter's denials of Jesus, when he was in the courtyard of the High Priest while Jesus was being questioned inside? From France:

> The later experience of Peter (26:69-75) is an object lesson in denying Jesus under the pressure of public opinion, but Peter's subsequent rehabilitation adds a reassuring suggestion that the stark verdict of this saying may be understood to refer to a settled course of acknowledgment or denial rather than to every temporary lapse under pressure.[170]

France puts forward the idea that 'one-off' occasions of denying allegiance to Jesus would be forgiven, but a long-lasting pattern of denials would not be forgiven: the person who keeps on denying Jesus Christ will not be acknowledged by Jesus before the Father. We must ask what Matthew is trying to say, when we link this passage (Mt 10:32-33) with Peter's denials of following Jesus; denying to the point of 'cursing (*katathematizein*)' (Mt 26:74; cf. Mk 14:71). Who or what did Peter curse?

> Does *katathematizein*, which we expect to be a transitive, have an implicit object – 'cursed (him)'? Most have suggested that Peter curses himself. But the best guess is that Jesus is the object of the curse: just as persecuted Christians were later on asked to curse Jesus and so dissociate themselves from their religion, so Peter here curses Jesus in an attempt to prove he is not a disciple.[171]

---

170 France, *Matthew*, 406.
171 W.D. Davies and Dale C. Allison, *A critical and exegetical commentary on the Gospel according to Saint Matthew*, Vol. 3, Matthew XIX-XXVIII (London/ New York: T&T Clark, 2004), 548-549. Also France, Matthew, 1034. "Matthew and Mark, by having the object unexpressed, refrain from stating in so many words that Peter cursed Jesus, but it is hard to see what else the choice of these transitive verbs could be meant to convey."

Does Matthew, as France proposes, 'rehabilitate' Peter in his Gospel? Rather, Peter – after denying Jesus, and cursing – exits the courtyard and goes out into the night. Are we meant to make a connection, that Peter is to join the company of those in the outer darkness because they have turned from God (Mt 8:12; 22:13; 25:30)? We are told that Peter "wept bitterly" (Mt 26:75), but are these tears of grief and repentance, or are they like the tears of those 'weeping and gnashing their teeth' (Mt 8:12; 13:42; 13:50; 22:13; 24:51; 25:30)? Matthew leaves us with a question mark about the extent of Peter's loyalty to Jesus, when he (Peter) is under pressure from Jesus' opponents.

Our last sight of Peter in this Gospel is of him leaving the courtyard (and Jesus) and going into the night (Mt 26:75. He is not named again for the rest of the Gospel, and is simply one of the unnamed eleven disciples who encounter the risen Jesus on the mountain in Galilee (Mt 28:16-17). Even here, when the disciples are face to face with Jesus, we are told that "some doubted (*hoi de edistasan*)." According to Matthew, is Peter one of those who still doubted?

Chapter Ten

The *mikros* and the *skandalon*. Matthew 18:1-35

Chapter eighteen (in which Jesus and Peter are the only two named speakers) can be read in general terms, about difficult situations which might arise in the Christian community; but underlying the whole chapter is, I believe, the relationship between Peter and Jacob in 62 C.E. This, then, is not so much a discourse from Jesus himself; it is a largely Matthean creation. The Evangelist writes this in the late sixties or seventies, knowing that Jacob and Peter have both died, but believing that the truth of a situation must somehow be recorded; perhaps to be revealed at a later time (Mt 10:26-27). I am dividing the chapter into five sections:

1. 18:1-6. Speaks of those who want to be considered the greatest in the kingdom of heaven, and those who cause 'little ones' to 'stumble' and sin.
2. 18:7-9. A 'Woe' to the one who is the cause of others stumbling and sinning.
3. 18:10-14. Speaks of the 'little one' who is not to be despised. This 'little one' is then metaphorically described as a sheep who strays from the flock, but is finally found by its shepherd.
4. 18:15-20. The steps to take if a 'brother' sins against you;

which may lead to some community members, or the whole community, being involved in the resolution of the situation.
5. 18:21-35. Peter's question to Jesus concerning the number of times his 'brother' should be forgiven for offending him. Jesus' response is to tell the story of the servant whose master forgives him for owing a huge debt, and releases him from that debt. The servant, in his turn, does not forgive a fellow servant who owes him a very small amount. The unforgiving servant finds himself sent to eternal torment.

The Greek words *mikros* ('little one'), *paidion* ('child'), *skandalon* (n) ('stumbling block'), and *skandalizō* (vb) ('cause someone to stumble') are all-important in this chapter. I associate Jacob with the 'little one' (*mikros*), and Peter ('Rock') with the *skandalon* who causes others to stumble. As said earlier, believe these (*mikros* and *skandalon*) are two of the main 'code words' in Matthew's Gospel, and are clues to what Matthew is saying behind the surface narrative.

Matthew 18:1-6

At that time the disciples came to Jesus, saying, "Who is the greatest in the kingdom of heaven?" And calling to him a child (*paidion*), he put him in the midst of them, and said, "Truly, I say to you, unless you turn and become like children (*paidia*), you will never enter the kingdom of heaven. Whoever humbles himself like this child (*to paidion touto*), he is the greatest in the kingdom of heaven. Whoever receives one such child (*hen paidion toiouto*) in my name receives me; but whoever causes one of these little ones (*hena tōn mikrōn toutōn*) who believe in me to sin (*skandalisē*), it would be better for him to have a great millstone fastened round his neck and to be drowned (*katapontisthē*) in the depth of the sea."

The idea of the disciples asking Jesus who of them will be greatest in the kingdom of heaven is not peculiar to Matthew's Gospel. Neither is it in Matthew's Gospel alone that Jesus is said to put a child 'in the midst' of the disciples (which we take to mean the Twelve chosen ones). We read a similar passage in Mark's Gospel:

> And they came to Capernaum; and when he was in the house he asked them, "What were you discussing on the way?" But they were silent; for on the way they had discussed with one another who was the greatest. And he sat down and called the twelve; and he said to them, "If any one would be first (*prōtos*), he must be last of all and servant of all." And he took a child (*paidion*), and put him in the midst of them; and taking him in his arms, he said to them, "Whoever receives one such child (*hen tōn toioutōn paidiōn*) in my name receives me; and whoever receives me, receives not me but him who sent me." (Mk 9:33-37)

Mark's account shows an intimacy between Jesus and the child, when Jesus is described as taking the child in his arms.

In Luke's parallel account we read:

> And an argument arose among them as to which of them was the greatest. But when Jesus perceived the thought of their hearts, he took a child (*paidion*) and put him by his side (*estēsen auto par heautō*), and said to them, "Whoever receives this child (*touto to paidion*) in my name receives me, and whoever receives me receives him who sent me; for he who is least (*mikroteros*) among you all is the one who is great. (Lk 9:46-48)

In Luke's account also, there is intimacy when Jesus takes the child and places him at his side. (We recall John's account of the last supper, when 'the disciple whom Jesus loved' (Jacob) was seated/reclining at Jesus' side (Jn 13:23).)[172] An indication that Luke has young

---

172 Katherine C. Linforth, *The Beloved Disciple: Jacob the Brother of the Lord* (Fremantle, W.A.: VIVID Publishing, 2014), 155-6.

Jacob in mind is his use of *mikroteros* (the one who is the least, the smallest) - a cognate of *mikros*. Matthew's account also brings in the word *mikros*: "whoever causes one of these little ones (*mikrōn*) who believe in me to sin, it would be better for him to have a great millstone fastened round his neck and to be drowned in the depth of the sea."

In Matthew 18:5, Mark 9:37 and Luke 9:48, Jesus says that anyone who receives one such child receives Jesus himself (and therefore receives the one who sent Jesus). This is extraordinary language: it could hardly mean receiving just any child. It has to be that the young child is the boy *Mikros* (Jacob). He is the specific child ('one such child') who is close to Jesus, and who is placed in the midst of the Twelve, with honour and respect. He is small, young, humble, and will grow up and become (following Peter's exit from Jerusalem[173]) the leader of the Christian Jewish community/ies for some twenty years. He was Jesus' brother, and in adulthood became known as 'Jacob the Righteous' for his piety and righteousness according to the Law. Jacob continued preaching and teaching his brother's message, and held the communities together while they waited for the return of Jesus the Messiah, Son of God. In Matthew's eyes, the *mikros* in this passage is the one who grew up to be, after Jesus, the 'greatest.'

In Mt 18:6 there is the stern warning to anyone who causes one of these little ones to sin:

> But whoever causes one of these little ones (*hena tōn mikrōn toutōn*) who believe in me to sin (*skandalisē*), it would be better for him to have a great millstone fastened round his neck and to be drowned (*katapontisthē*) in the depth of the sea.

Here we may have a reference to Peter (Rock), the one who causes Jacob (*Mikros*) to trip up (*skandalisē*). (The 'trip' may be taken

---

[173] Acts 12:17.

as both metaphorical – that Jacob transgressed the Law in some way - and literal, in that Jacob was made to fall from the wing of the temple.) The millstone around the neck is suitable for one who is himself a stone/rock. To drown would be preferable to facing the judgement of God and being thrown into the eternal hell of fire (Mt 18:8-9). The only other place in this Gospel where the verb *katapontizō* is found is at Matthew 14:30, when Peter begins to walk on the waters towards Jesus; but 'seeing the wind' he begins to sink (*katapontizesthai*).

Matthew 18:7-12

Woe to the world for temptations to sin (*skandalōn*)! For it is necessary that temptations (*skandala*) come, but woe to the man by whom the temptation (*skandalon*) comes! And if your hand or your foot causes you to sin (*skandalizei*), cut it off and throw it from you; it is better for you to enter life maimed or lame than with two hands or two feet to be thrown into the eternal fire. And if your eye causes you to sin (*skandalizei*), pluck it out and throw it from you; it is better for you to enter life with one eye than with two eyes to be thrown into the hell of fire.

What do we make of these verses? There are five cognates of *skandalon/skandalizei*. In other words, 'tripping up' is repeated again and again in these verses. I believe Matthew is emphasising his case against Peter ('Rock'): the one who has tripped up Jacob is to be himself thrown into the hell of fire, unless he roots out that aspect of himself ('hand,' 'foot,' eye') which makes him a *skandalon*.

Matthew 18:10-14

See that you do not despise one of these little ones (*henōs ton mikrōn toutōn*); for I tell you that in heaven their angels always behold the face of my Father who is in heaven. What do you think? If a man has a hundred sheep, and one of them has gone astray, does he not leave

the ninety-nine on the hills and go in search of the one that went astray? And if he finds it, truly, I say to you, he rejoices over it more than over the ninety-nine that never went astray. So it is not the will of my Father who is in heaven that one of these little ones (*hen tōn mikrōn toutōn*) should perish.

This passage is another Matthean 'sandwich,' as the phrase 'one of these little ones' is at the beginning and the end of it. The warning is not to despise (*kataphronēsēte*) one of these little ones. "Despising connotes both an attitude of disdainfulness and injurious acts growing out of that attitude (see 6:24; Luke 16:13; 1 Cor 11:22; 1 Tim 4:12)."[174]

We are told that the angels of these little ones always behold the face of God the Father (Mt 18:10):

> The last clause refers to the little ones' angels, a theological notion that stems from the tradition reflected in Luke 15:10 and tallies with Matthew's distinctive doctrines of the angels of the Son of man (13:41; 16:27; 24:31; 25:31; 26:53) and the Devil's angels (25:41). As in these other passages, so also here the angels aid those they belong to.[175]

Matthew is telling us that, because the little one's angels are always in the Father's presence, the Father always has the little one in his ongoing care.

Now, in Matthew 18:12-13, there is a sudden switch, from a warning not to despise one of the little ones to a story about a sheep which is straying. The sheep is straying, not because it is lost, but because it has wandered away from its shepherd and fellow sheep. We imagine a member of the community drifting away from the

---

[174] Robert H. Gundry, *Matthew: A Commentary on His Handbook for a Mixed Church under Persecution*, 2nd ed. (Grand Rapids, Michigan: William B. Eerdmans, 1994), 364.

[175] Gundry, *Matthew: Commentary*, 364.

community, and from Jesus, who has brought the community into being. If we take this sheep as alluding to the adult Jacob (*Mikros*), it would seem that Matthew finds fault not only with Peter but with Jacob. Jacob the Righteous, according to Matthew, has also strayed from the Way of Jesus.

There is an interesting Logion in the Gospel of Thomas[176] which may reflect this Matthean passage.

> Jesus said, "The kingdom is like a shepherd who had a hundred sheep. One of them, the largest, went astray. He left the ninety-nine and looked for that one until he found it. When he had gone to such trouble, he said to the sheep, 'I care for you more than the ninety-nine.'"[177] (*Gospel of Thomas*, Logion 107)

What would anyone have made of this saying which has no context? But I believe we know the hidden story, through Matthew's Gospel, and so for us the Logion springs to life. As in Matthew's account, the (one) sheep 'went astray'; that is, Jacob the Righteous was said to have done something contrary to the Law, resulting in him being charged with transgressing the Law. The sheep in the Logion is 'the largest' – that is, the most important one. Jacob was the leader of the Christian Jewish communities for twenty or more years; he was 'number one' - the 'largest' in terms of authority and leadership. Moreover, he was Jesus' brother; the 'disciple whom Jesus loved' of John's Gospel.

---

176 "The Gospel of Thomas," in *The Other Bible*, Willis Barnstone, ed. (New York: HarperSanFrancisco, 2005), 299. "The *Gospel of Thomas* is a collection of traditional sayings, prophecies, proverbs, and parables of Jesus. The Coptic *Gospel of Thomas* was translated from the Greek; in fact, several fragments of this Greek version have been preserved, and can be dated to about A.D. 200."

177 Barnstone, *Other Bible*, 307.

Matthew 18:15-20

If your brother sins against you, go (*hupage*) and tell him his fault, between you and him alone. If he listens to you, you have gained your brother. But if he does not listen, take one or two others along with you, that every word may be confirmed by the evidence of two or three witnesses. If he refuses to listen to them, tell it to the church; and if he refuses to listen even to the church, let him be to you as a Gentile and a tax collector. Truly, I say to you, whatever you bind on earth shall be bound in heaven, and whatever you loose on earth shall be loosed in heaven. Again I say to you, if two of you agree on earth about anything they ask, it will be done for them by my Father in heaven. For where two or three are gathered in my name, there am I in the midst of them.

Matthew is spelling out what a member of the community should do if a 'brother' in the community sins against him or her. Is Matthew also explaining what Peter *should* have done, when he and Jacob exchanged harsh words? The first step would be to have a private conversation with the brother, talking about the perceived offence. If there is no reconciliation, then the injured party is to take two or three other community members to meet with the offender. However, if even this small group meeting fails to bring about reconciliation, then the whole community meets to hear the complaint, and to decide a course of action. This may lead to the exclusion of the offender from the community ("let him be to you as a Gentile and a tax collector").

This is the way to resolve disputes, according to the Matthean Jesus. In Matthew 18:15 Jesus tells the offended member of the community: "Go (*hupage*)." The offended one is to find his 'brother' and talk about the perceived offence, with the aim of reconciling with him. As Gundry says: "The instruction of *hupage* conforms to Matthew's diction and puts the onus of responsibility on the brother sinned against; 'go!'"[178] We find this imperative 'Go' elsewhere in Matthew's Gospel. We have noted it in Matthew 5:23-24, where the person bringing a gift to the altar is told that they must leave the gift, and *go (hupage)* and be reconciled with the one who has something against the gift-bringer.

In Matthew 16:15-17, Peter has been lauded by Jesus for Peter's acknowledgement of Jesus as "the Christ, the Son of the living God." Jesus adds that he (Jesus) will build his church on this "rock *(petra)*," and "the powers of hell shall not prevail against it" (Mt 16:18). Yet within a very short time Peter 'rebukes' Jesus, who turns and says to Peter, "Get behind me, Satan *(hupage opisō mou, satana)*! You are a hindrance *(skandalon)* to me; for you are not on the side of God, but of men" (Mt 16:23).

With these three instances of 'Go *(hupage)*' I believe that Matthew intends us to 'connect the dots' - to understand that the offended one (Mt 18:15; cf. Mt 5:22-24) who is to seek reconciliation with his 'brother' is Peter.

Matthew 18:21-22

Then Peter came up and said to him, "Lord, how often shall my brother sin against me, and I forgive him? As many as seven times?" Jesus said to him, "I do not say to you seven times, but seventy times seven."

We finally have a named (not hypothetical) member of the community who speaks of being sinned against by his brother - and it is Peter. This episode of Peter approaching Jesus and asking him how often he (Peter) is to forgive his brother who has wronged him, is, I believe, Matthew's allusion to angry words exchanged between Peter and Jacob (Mt 5:21-22).

Peter, in Matthew 18:21, is willing to forgive his brother up to

---

178 Gundry, *Matthew: Commentary*, 367.

seven times.[179] Seven times is a considerable number of times to forgive a brother, but Jesus responds by saying that forgiveness is required seventy-seven times (which in effect means an unlimited number of times). For Matthew's readers/hearers who were familiar with the book of Exodus, the phrase 'seventy-seven times' brings up the name of Lamech (Gen 4:18-24). Lamech is a rather mysterious character: he is a descendant of Cain, who slew his own brother Abel. Lamech speaks of his own vengeance, to the extent of seventy-times seven. He says to his wives, Adah and Zillah:

> Adah and Zillah, hear my voice; you wives of Lamech,
> listen to what I say: I have killed a man for wounding me,
> a young man for striking me. If Cain is avenged sevenfold,
> truly Lamech is seventy-sevenfold. (Gen 4:23-24. NRSV)

This Lamech story is without context, but is Matthew, the one who knew scripture so well, alluding to a desire in Peter for vengeance against Jacob (a young man who 'wounded' him)?

Earlier in the Gospel Jesus has given his disciples a promise and a warning. Forgiveness, given through the mercy of God, must also be extended by those who have been 'offended' by the actions or words of others: "For if you forgive men (*anthrōpoi* [180]) their trespasses, your heavenly Father also will forgive you; but if you do not forgive men (*anthrōpoi*) their trespasses, neither will your Father forgive your trespasses" (Mt 6:14-15).

Mathew 18:23-25

Jesus immediately follows his command of unreserved forgiveness with the story of the king and the two servants. (The story is

---

[179] In Luke 17:3-4, a parallel pericope, Jesus tells his disciples that they are to forgive a brother seven times in the one day, after the brother says, '"I repent." The Matthean Jesus says the brother is to be forgiven seventy-seven times; there is no mention of repentance on the brother's part.

[180] *anthrōpoi*. Does not mean 'men,' in its biological sense, but rather 'persons,' 'human beings.'

printed in full in Chapter Five of this present work.) A king wishes to settle his accounts, and asks one of his servants to repay a loan of ten thousand talents – an enormous sum. The servant is unable to repay the loan, and the king orders that the servant, with his wife and children, be sold, as payment for the debt. The servant pleads for more time to repay, whereupon the king - 'filled with tenderness (*splanchnistheis*[181])' - releases him from his debt.

On leaving the king's presence, the servant encounters a fellow servant who owes him a small amount of money, and demands that the debt be repaid. The fellow servant pleads for patience, so that he can repay the debt, but the first servant has him put in prison until the debt is repaid. The first servant's actions are reported to the king by other, deeply distressed servants, and the first servant is brought back before the king. The king tells him: "You wicked servant! I forgave you all that debt because you besought me; and should not you have had mercy on your fellow servant, as I had mercy on you?" (Mt 18:32-33). The first servant is then delivered to the 'jailers (*basanistais* = 'torturers/tormenters')' until he can pay his debt – an impossible task.

Jesus ends this story with a warning to all his listeners, not just to Peter: "So also my heavenly Father will do to every one of you, if you do not forgive your brother from your heart" (Mt 18:35).

I believe that this story is Matthew's response to the situation between Peter and Jacob in 62 C.E. If Peter is represented by the first servant (who seems to hold a position of consequence in the king's palace), what is his great 'debt'? For what would Peter need to be forgiven? Surely for his denials of knowing 'the man' (that is, Jesus) and of cursing (cursing Jesus?) and swearing, when confronted by servants and bystanders in the high priest's courtyard (Mt 26:69-74).

181　Vb *splanchnizomai*. 'have compassion,' 'have pity.'

His denials and curses would be an enormous 'debt,'[182] and yet in Matthew's story the king (God) is 'filled with tenderness.' He releases the first servant from all debt, and forgives him (Mt 18:27).

The second servant, who owes the first servant a small amount of money, pleads with the first servant for more time to repay the debt, but the first servant refuses, and has the second servant put in prison (Mt 18:29-30). If the second servant represents Jacob, did Jacob ask for Peter's forgiveness after they quarrelled? Did Peter refuse to forgive Jacob, and so initiate a train of events which led to Jacob being taken to the Sanhedrin on a charge of transgressing the Law? There were many of the hierarchy who would have welcomed a means of getting rid of Jacob.

The fellow servants in this story represent the Christian (and non-Christian) Jews of Jerusalem and elsewhere around the Mediterranean, who would have been stunned and grief-stricken at the public execution of Jesus' brother, Jacob the Righteous.

The ending, where the first servant is "delivered to the jailers ('torturers')" (Mt 18:34) is a grim warning. Was Matthew, writing in the sixties or seventies, imagining Peter's last days in Rome, when he would most probably have been tortured, before being executed?

---

182 France, *Matthew*, 703. "This story about monetary debt picks up the language of 6:12, which uses 'debt' for the sin which needs to be forgiven. This parable thus spells out what Jesus has stated in stark propositional form in his comment on 6:12 in 6:14-15, that forgiveness must be reciprocal, so that God cannot be expected to forgive the unforgiving."

Chapter Eleven

Between the sanctuary and the altar. Matthew 23:29-37a

This narrative of Jesus' seventh and final 'Woe' against the scribes and Pharisees, is, I believe, giving us a snapshot of Jacob's death. In this Gospel there have been earlier allusions to Jacob's death, beginning with Matthew 4:5-6, when the devil invites Jesus to throw himself down from the pinnacle (*pterugion* = 'little wing') of the temple (see Chapter Five of this present work). The promise is that angels will bear him up, "lest you strike your foot against a stone."

In Chapter Nine of this present work I explored the imagery of the 'sparrow' (*strouthion* = 'little bird') falling to the ground, after being struck by a fowler's weapon (Mt 10:29). The 'little bird' is, I believe, a reference to Jacob (*Mikros*), who died after being thrown from a height, then was stoned and had his head beaten in with a club. My question all the way through this present work has been: does Matthew believe that Peter was the 'fowler' who brought about the death of Jacob?

Here in Matthew 23:29-37a, I believe we have an allusion to the place where Jacob died, and to the manner in which he died.

Woe to you, scribes and Pharisees, hypocrites! for you build the tombs of the prophets and adorn the monuments

of the righteous (*dikaiōn*), saying, "If we had lived in the days of our fathers, we would not have taken part with them in shedding the blood of the prophets." Thus you witness against yourselves, that you are sons of those who murdered the prophets. Fill up, then, the measure of your fathers. You serpents, you brood of vipers, how are you to escape being sentenced to hell? Therefore I send you prophets and wise men and scribes,[183] some of whom you will kill and crucify, and some you will scourge in your synagogues and persecute from town to town, that upon you may come all the righteous blood (*pan haima dikaion*) shed on earth, from the blood of innocent Abel (*Abel tou dikaiou* = 'Abel the righteous'[184]) to the blood of Zechariah the son of Barachiah, whom you murdered between the sanctuary (*naou*) and the altar. Truly, I say to you, all this will come upon this generation. O Jerusalem, Jerusalem, killing the prophets and stoning those who are sent to you! (Mt 23:29-37a)**

This passage raises several questions for biblical scholars. Most agree that the references to 'righteous blood,' with the examples of the murders of Abel and Zechariah, form sort of book-ends in Hebrew scripture.[185] Abel's death – by the hand of his brother – is the first one

---

183 The 'scribes' that Jesus sends, after his death and resurrection, will surely include Jacob ('the letter of James'), Paul (his letters), Peter (two letters in his name, although the authenticity of the second letter is generally disputed), and the other writers in the New Testament, such as Mark, Luke and John.

184 Abel is described as 'righteous' in Heb 11:4 and 1 Jn 3:12. The latter (which I believe to be written by Jacob himself) says: "For this is the message which you have heard from the beginning, that we should love one another, and not be like Cain who was of the evil one and murdered his brother. And why did he murder him? Because his own deeds were evil and his brother's righteous."

185 R.T. France, *The Gospel of Matthew* (Grand Rapids, Michigan: William B. Eerdmans, 2007), 880. "The tradition of the murder of the righteous

recorded (Gen 4:8). The death of Zechariah (the Zechariah whose father was Jehoida, not Barachiah) in the temple was at the hands of fellow Israelites, and is recorded in 2 Chronicles 24:20-22.

Davies and Allison point out the difficulty with this accusation by Jesus (Mt 28:29-30):

> Why does the recompense due for the murders of all the righteous come down upon only one group? The question is often asked, especially as (i) the scribes and Pharisees had nothing to do with the murder of Zechariah and (ii) no Israelite had anything to do with Abel's murder.[186]

Why indeed is Jesus accusing the scribes and Pharisees of murdering Zechariah, who lived some hundreds of years earlier? I believe that this is actually Matthew's accusation against the scribes and Pharisees of his own day, that they murdered Jacob – Jacob the Righteous. Matthew is using the name 'Zechariah son of Barachiah' as a means of speaking about Jacob.

The prophet Zechariah introduces himself as 'Zechariah, son of Berechiah' (Zech 1.1), yet this Zechariah didn't die a violent death at the hands of others. The most likely Zechariah, in terms of Matthew's description of his being stoned to death within the temple, is Zechariah son of Jehoida, who was stoned to death "in the court of the house of the Lord" (2 Chr 24:20-21). I believe that Matthew has not made a mistake in writing "Zechariah son of Barachiah" but is leading us to the realisation that it is Jacob about whom he is writing. Barachiah means 'blessed by God,' and for Matthew it would be Jacob

---

is traced from the first to the last such deaths recorded in the OT, that of Abel in Gen 4:8 and that of Zechariah in 2 Chr 24:20-22. The death of Zechariah in the late ninth century B.C. was of course not the last martyrdom in historical sequence, but because it is recorded toward the end of 2 Chronicles, the last book of the Hebrew canon, it suitably rounds off the biblical record of God's servants killed for their loyalty."

186 W.D. Davies and Dale C. Allison, *A Critical and Exegetical Commentary on the Gospel according to Saint Matthew*, Vol. 3, Matthew XIX-XXVIII (London/New York: T&T Clark, 2004), 317.

who was 'blessed by God.'

Both Zechariah son of Jehoida and Jacob, Jesus' brother, were killed within the temple complex: Zechariah son of Jehoida was stoned "in the court of the house of the Lord," and Matthew tells us that Zechariah son of Barachiah was killed "between the sanctuary and the altar" (Mt 23:35). The location is so specific, it must surely be something that Matthew knew from personal knowledge, or from reports of Jacob's death.

Abel was killed out of jealousy and resentment by his brother Cain. In this present work I am putting forward the theory that Matthew believed Peter to be responsible for Jacob's death, because of his (Peter's) ongoing resentment of Jacob; that Jacob's death came about because Peter criticised Jacob to someone else, and that someone communicated it to the Jerusalem hierarchy, which then set in process the events leading to Jacob's execution. Peter was not Jacob's biological brother in the way that Cain was the biological brother of Abel, but he was very much a 'brother in Christ,' as the two men had known each other since Jacob was a boy (Gal 1:18-19)[187].

Jesus most probably did predict the persecution of his followers in later years (Mt 23:34), but in this passage I believe the words are those of Matthew himself, remembering the persecutions and martyrdoms of the previous decades. We know the names of some of those who were martyred, post c30 C.E. Stephen was stoned to death in the thirties (Acts 6 and 7); James of Zebedee died by the sword in the early forties (Acts 12:1-2a); Jacob, the brother of Jesus, was killed in Jerusalem in 62 C.E.; Peter and Paul died in Rome in the sixties. We know, from Paul's letters and from Acts, of the persecution which he suffered throughout his ministry.

The last sentence of Matthew 23:37a is a lament by Jesus: "O

---

187 Katherine C. Linforth, *The Beloved Disciple: Jacob the Brother of the Lord* (Fremantle, W.A.: VIVID Publishing, 2014), 36-37.

Jerusalem, Jerusalem, killing the prophets and stoning those who are sent to you!" He was not speaking only of what had happened in the past, but what was still to take place.

> Jesus speaks first of what the inhabitants of the city have done in the past. Jerusalem is the city that kills the prophets and stones God's messengers (the present participles point not to an occasional aberration, but to the continuing practice.[188]

For Matthew, the scribes and Pharisees are the ones who bear the guilt and shame of murdering Jesus' brother, Jacob.

---

[188] Leon Morris, *The Gospel according to Matthew* (Grand Rapids, Michigan: William B. Eerdmans/Leicester, U.K.: Inter-Varsity Press, 1992), 590.

– Chapter Twelve –

The redemption and death of Peter. Matthew 14:22-33

Introduction

Throughout this present work I have been working to uncover a story which I believe Matthew has hidden within the story of Jesus Christ. It is the story of Simon Peter and Jacob, Jesus' brother, at the time of the Passover festival in Jerusalem in 62 C.E. In the previous chapter we explored what I believe is Matthew's referencing of the place of Jacob's death – "murdered between the sanctuary and the altar" (Mt 23:35). Now, looking at a story which is at the literal, physical centre of Matthew's Gospel, we will explore what I believe is Matthew's symbolic depiction of Peter's redemption, and death, in Rome in 64 C.E.

Background to the persecution in Rome

Peter is believed to have died in Rome in the weeks or months after the great fire of July, 64 C.E. The fire, which lasted for days, destroyed large areas of the city, making many people homeless. At some point a rumour started, saying that the emperor Nero was responsible for the fire; this, it was said, was in order to acquire land on which to build himself an incredibly large palace with extensive grounds and

gardens. Tacitus[189] says:
> Wherefore to efface the rumour, Nero contrived that accusations should be brought against a set of people hated for their abominations, whom the populace called Christians, and subjected them to the most exquisite torments.[190]
>
> Those therefore who confessed were first brought to trial, afterwards by the information derived from them, an immense multitude were joined with them, not so much for the crime of incendiarism, as for hatred of the human race.[191]

The 'information' was no doubt gained by torture, or the threat of torture. In Matthew's Gospel we hear warnings that people will betray each other in times of persecution. Although the apparent context would seem to be Israel, I believe Matthew may have had the Neronian persecution of Christians in mind:
> Brother will deliver up brother to death, and the father his child, and children will rise against parents and have them put to death; and you will be hated by all for my name's sake. (Mt 10:21-22a)
>
> Then they will deliver you up to tribulation, and put you to death; and you will be hated by all nations for my name's sake. And then many will fall away, and betray one another, and hate one another. (Mt 24:9-10))

The treatment meted out to the Christians in Rome who were taken into custody was savage. Tacitus writes:
> To their deaths mockeries were added, so that covered by the skins of wild beasts they were torn to pieces by dogs and

---

189 Publius Cornelius Tacitus (c56-120 C.E.), Roman historian and politician.
190 George Edmundson, *The Church in Rome in the First Century* (London: Longmans, Green and Co., 1913), 124.
191 Edmundson, *Church in Rome*, 128.

perished or were affixed to crosses or set on fire and, when day had fallen, were burnt so as to serve as an illumination for the night. Nero had offered his gardens for the spectacle, and was exhibiting a public show in the circus.[192] He mingled with the people in the dress of a charioteer, standing in a car. Hence compassion began to arise, although towards criminals deserving the extremest forms of punishment, on the ground that they were destroyed not for the public good but to gratify a single man's savage cruelty.[193]

This was the time when Peter was (most probably) crucified and then burned to death.[194] Simon Peter, as the 'first,' most well-known of Jesus' disciples, must surely have been one of the targets – the principal target? – of Nero's persecution of Christians in Rome.

Matthew 14:22-33

This episode of Peter starting to walk on the waters towards Jesus, is, for me, Matthew's narrative of Peter's 'redemption and death,'[195] written after Peter's martyrdom. So much of Matthew's Gospel is concerned with Peter's weaknesses; the foremost being Peter's enthusiastic vow of loyalty to Jesus (Mt 26:33-35) which is followed

---

192 The circus (built by Caligula) was Nero's hippodrome, a rectangular structure used for chariot-racing. A low wall, called the *spina*, ran down the centre, with space left at each end for the racing chariots to make the turns. Nero's circus was west of the Tiber river, in the location of the present-day St Peter's Basilica, and is regarded as the site of the martyrdom of Peter and the other Christians.

193 Edmundson, *Church in Rome*, 128.

194 An article by Timothy D. Barnes puts forward that Simon Peter was burned alive, rather than dying by crucifixion. I believe there is evidence in John's Gospel that supports Barnes' theory. See Timothy D. Barnes, "Another shall gird thee," in *Peter in Early Christianity*, Helen K. Bond and Larry Hurtado, eds. (Grand Rapids, Michigan/Cambridge, U.K.: William B. Eerdmans, 2015), 76-95.

195 Comparable in some ways to John's story of the 'redemption and death' of Peter (Jn 21:7-19).

not long after by Peter's failure (three times) to profess publicly his discipleship of Jesus (Mt 26:69-75). Even more than those overt instances of Peter's failure, I believe Matthew has in mind the death of Jesus' brother Jacob, which Matthew believes came about through Peter's inability to keep his anger to himself.

In Matthew 14:22-33 I see the Evangelist describing, in a symbolic way, the last days of Simon Peter's life. Matthew has placed this story at the literal centre of his Gospel: he has added his own material to the parallel stories found in Mark 6:45-52 and John 6:15-21. Neither of these parallel stories names Peter; the disciples are a unit, without a spokesperson.

In the 'hidden' story of Peter in Matthew 14:22-33, Peter emerges as a heroic figure who, recognising his own weaknesses, calls out to Jesus for help, and is saved. Let us look closely at Matthew 14:22-33, to find what I believe supports my theory that Matthew is speaking of Peter's redemption and death.

> **Then he [Jesus] made the disciples get into the boat and go before him to the other side, while he dismissed the crowds. And after he had dismissed the crowds, he went up into the hills by himself to pray. When evening came, he was there alone, but the boat by this time was many furlongs distant from the land, beaten by the waves; for the wind was against them. And in the fourth watch of the night he came to them, walking on the sea. But when the disciples saw him walking on the sea, they were terrified, saying, "It is a ghost!" And they cried out for fear. But immediately he spoke to them, saying, "Take heart, it is I; have no fear." And Peter answered him, "Lord, if it is you, bid me come to you on the water." He said, "Come." So Peter got out of the boat and walked on the water and came to Jesus; but when he saw the wind he was afraid, and beginning to sink he cried out, "Lord, save me." Jesus immediately reached out his hand and**

caught him, saying to him, "O man of little faith, why did you doubt?" And when they got into the boat, the wind ceased. And those in the boat worshiped him, saying, "Truly you are the Son of God." (Mt 14:22-33)

R.T. France points out that, "The situation seems to be similar to the storm in 8:24, though the focus in this narrative is on the wind (vv. 24, 30, 32) rather than the waves."[196] Here the powerful wind, blowing contrary to the direction in which the boat is heading, represents the climate of terror in Rome because of Nero's active persecution of Christians; persecution which encompasses betrayal, torture, and death as public entertainment in Nero's stadium. Let us look at the narrative in small sections, to see how Matthew alludes to the story behind the Jesus story.

Matthew 14:22
Then he made (*ēnankazen*[197]) the disciples get into the boat and go before him to the other side, while he dismissed the crowds.

As night falls, Jesus orders his disciples to get into the boat and go to the other side, while he is alone on the mountain in prayer. We are not told where 'the other side' is, so the reader assumes it is the other side of the Sea of Galilee. But Matthew is not indicating a literal 'other side' of the Sea of Galilee; the 'other side' is the other side of the Mediterranean Sea, in Rome.

The disciples are given no choice about leaving Jesus alone. Jesus makes them get into the boat and go to another place. Where else in this Gospel does Jesus send away his disciples? It is at the very end

---

196 R.T. France, *The Gospel of Matthew* (Grand Rapids, Michigan; Cambridge, U.K.:William B. Eerdmans, 2007), 569.

197 W.D. Davies and Dale C. Allison, *A Critical and Exegetical Commentary on the Gospel according to Saint Matthew*, Vol. 2, Matthew VIII-XVIII (London/New York: T&T Clark, 2004), 501. "αναγκαζω (= 'compel', 'force') is used only three times in the synoptics, in Mt 14:22=Mk 6:45 and in Lk 14:23.

of the Gospel, when the remaining eleven disciples encounter the risen Jesus, who tells them: "Go therefore and make disciples of all nations" (Mt 28:19). After Jesus' death and resurrection the disciples *have* gone out, and Rome is one of places (perhaps one of the earliest) where Christianity has been established. So the boat, with its disciples, represents the Christian community/communities in Rome.

Matthew 14:23

And after he had dismissed the crowds, he went up (*anebē*[198]) into the hills (*eis to horos* = 'into the mountain') by himself to pray. When evening came, he was there alone

Jesus is alone on the mountain after the disciples have gone; but knowing how Matthew conflates ideas, actual events, and periods of time, we should understand that when Jesus 'goes up' the image is that of Jesus being lifted up on the cross, where he prays.[199] We know of his prayer, from Matthew 27:46:

And about the ninth hour Jesus cried with a loud voice, "*Eli, Eli, la'ma sabach-tha'-ni?*" that is, "My God, my God, why hast thou forsaken me?"

Jesus at that point expresses his belief (?), fear (?) that God has deserted him - has left him alone in his agony and dying. He doesn't lose faith in the existence of God, but thinks that perhaps God has left him to his fate. Similarly, many of the Christians (those in the 'boat') in Rome, during the Neronian persecution, would have been experiencing that same terror, and the same fear that God had abandoned them in their suffering.

---

198 Vb *anabainō*. 'ascend,' 'go up.' This verb is used in John's Gospel when Jesus ascends to his Father (Jn 3:13; 6:62; 20:17).

199 Donald A. Hagner, *Matthew 14-28* (Dallas, Texas: Word Books, c1995), 422. "The other references to Jesus praying (προσευχεσθαι) in Matthew are in 26:36, 39, 42, 44 (cf. Luke 9:28), all in connection with his own imminent suffering and death."

Matthew 14:24

but the boat by this time was many furlongs (*stadious pollous*) distant from the land, beaten (*basanizomenon*) by the waves; for the wind was against them.

The 'many furlongs' are 'many *stadia*,' in the Greek. The *stadion* (about 185 metres long) was a Roman measurement of distance, and no doubt it became the standard measure of distance for the inhabitants of occupied Galilee and elsewhere. But here Matthew could just as easily have said that the boat was a 'great distance' from the land.[200] However, he uses the word *stadia*, with its connotations of Roman culture, and of the city of Rome itself. 'Many *stadia*' has the connotation of a great distance.

Even more significantly, Nero had a stadium[201] – a hippodrome for chariot-racing – in which so many Christians were publicly tortured and put to death.[202] (This was not the Circus Maximus, which was destroyed in the fire, but Nero's private hippodrome west of the Tiber.) So Matthew's use of the word *stadia* might not only be alluding to the distance from Galilee to Rome, but also to Nero's 'stadium.'

The strong wind is a head wind. The 'wind' is the forcefulness of Nero's edict to target Christians, ostensibly for setting a fire that destroyed large areas of Rome. The 'boat' (the Church in Rome) is being beaten and buffeted by the waves, so that the boat and those in it are being thrown up and down and from side to side, while all the time

---

200 In Mark 6:47 (Gk) the boat is 'in the midst of the sea'; in John 6:19 (Gk) the boat has covered a distance of 25 or 30 *stadia*.

201 The Latinized form of the Greek *stadion*. 'Stadium' came to mean the actual place of the games.

202 "Circus of Nero." Wikipedia. Accessed 15 November, 2024. en.wikipedia.org/wiki/Circus_of_Nero. "The site for crucifixions in the Circus would have been along the *spina* (spine), as suggested by the 2nd century Acts of Peter describing the spot of his martyrdom as *inter duas metas* (between the two metal or turning posts), which would have been equidistant between the two ends of the Circus."

the strong wind blows. According to Leon Morris, "βασανιζω may be used in the sense 'torture,' and from that it comes to signify any severe distress. Here the waves are pictured as harassing the sailors."[203] I take this image of the boat being 'tortured' by the waves as representing the actual torture that would have taken place in Rome, in order to make Christians betray other Christians. As Matthew writes elsewhere (picking up on Mark 13:12): "Brother will deliver up brother to death, and the father his child, and children will rise against parents and have them put to death" (Mt 10:21; cf. Mt 24:9-10).

The violence of the wind and waves pictures what I believe is in Matthew's mind; the scene of what happened post-harvesting, when the threshing and winnowing of the harvested crops took place. Earlier in his Gospel Matthew has spoken (through the words of John the Baptist) of the time of judgement as a time of threshing and winnowing:

> His winnowing fork is in his hand, and he will clear his threshing floor and gather his wheat into the granary, but the chaff he will burn with unquenchable fire. (Mt 3:12)

Just as the grain was separated, first by threshing,[204] and then by winnowing,[205] the Neronian persecution was a 'threshing and

---

203 Leon Morris, *The Gospel according to Matthew* (Grand Rapids, Michigan: William B. Eerdmans/Cambridge, U.K.: Inter-Varsity Press, 1992), 381. Footnote 55.

204 H.N. Richardson, "Threshing," in *The Interpreter's Dictionary of the Bible*, Vol. R-Z, George Arthur Buttrick, ed. (Nashville, Abingdon, 1962), 636. "The stalks were laid out on a threshing floor, a flat surface of rock or pounded earth located in an open place exposed to the wind ... Several different methods of threshing were used ... One of these ... was a frame with rollers into which were fastened sharp stones or pieces of metal (Isa 28:27-28). Another machine ... was made of planks turned up a little at the front with sharp stones or pieces of metal fixed into holes bored in the bottom. These machines were pulled by animals around and around over the grain."

205 H.N. Richardson, "Winnowing," in *The Interpreter's Dictionary of the Bible*, Vol. R-Z, George Arthur Buttrick, ed. (Nashville: Abingdon, 1962), 852. "The process of throwing the cut stalks of grain into the air so that the

winnowing' of the Christians in Rome, separating the loyal followers of Jesus Christ from those who recanted (either because they doubted that Jesus was Son of God (Messiah/Christos), or because of their fear of torture and death).

A passage from Luke's Gospel is relevant here. In the course of the last supper, Jesus speaks to his disciples of the forthcoming persecution which they will face; then Jesus speaks directly to Simon (Peter):

> Simon, Simon, behold, Satan demanded to have you [pl.], that he might sift you [pl.] like wheat, but I have prayed for you [sg.] that your [sg.] faith may not fail; and when you [sg.] have turned [again], strengthen your [sg.] brethren.
> (Lk 22:31-32)

At this point Simon[206] (Peter) declares his willingness to go with Jesus to prison and to death (Lk 22:33). Is Luke also, in retrospect, giving us a glimpse of Peter's final days? That Peter would turn aside from following Jesus at a time when fellow Christians needed 'strengthening'? That he would turn again, to follow Jesus, and 'strengthen' his Christian brothers and sisters? If this is the case, there may be a factual foundation to the *Quo Vadis?* ('Where are you going?') story, as related in The Acts of Peter.[207]

And the rest of the brethren together with Marcellus

---

kernels will fall into a pile and the refuse will be carried away by the wind. Winnowing follows threshing (Isa 41:15-16). At the beginning of the work a fork is used and later a shovel (Isa 30:24). It is done on the threshing floor in the late afternoon and evening, when the wind will be blowing (Ruth 3:2). As the stalks are tossed, the grain falls at the workers' feet, the straw is carried a short distance, and the chaff is often blown beyond the borders of the threshing floor (Mat 3:12)."

206 Note the use of the name 'Simon,' not 'Peter.' John's Gospel, in particular, uses 'Simon' for the 'good' Peter, but 'Peter (Rock)' is used when Peter is being obstructive or causes trouble to others; in other words, acting like a *skandalon*.

207 "The Acts of Peter," in *The Other Bible*, Rev. ed., Willis Barnstone, ed. (New York: HarperSanFrancisco, 2005).

entreated him [Peter] to withdraw [from Rome]. But Peter said to them, "Shall we act like deserters, brethren?" But they said to him, "No, it is so that you can go on serving the Lord." So he assented to the brethren and withdrew by himself, saying, "Let none of you retire with me, but I shall retire by myself in disguise." And as he went out of the gate he saw the Lord entering Rome; and when he saw him he said, "Lord, where are you going?" And the Lord said to him, "I am coming to Rome to be crucified." And Peter said to him, "Lord, are you being crucified again?" He said to him, "Yes, Peter, I am being crucified again." And Peter came to himself; and he saw the Lord ascending into heaven; then he returned to Rome, rejoicing and giving praise to the Lord, because he said, "I am being crucified"; since this was to happen to Peter.[208]

That Peter underwent significant suffering (torture) in Rome is mentioned in a letter attributed to Clement of Rome:

Through resentment and envy the greatest and most righteous "pillars" were persecuted and contended unto death. Let us set before our eyes the good apostles – Peter, who because of unrighteous resentment experienced not one or two but many afflictions; and after giving his testimony in this fashion, he went to the place of glory that was his due.[209]

---

208 *Other Bible*, 442.
209 Markus Bockmuehl, *Simon Peter in Scripture and Memory* (Grand Rapids, Michigan: Baker Academic, 2012), 109. As to the dating of the letter, Bockmuehl says, "The conventional scholarly consensus regards the anonymously authored document known as *1 Clement* as a letter written around the year AD 96, although there are also arguments favoring an earlier date around the year AD 70 (others claim a date as late as Hadrian)." (Bockmuehl, *Simon Peter*, 108.)

> **Matthew 14:25-27**
> **And in the fourth watch of the night he came to them, walking on the sea (*thalassan*). But when the disciples saw him walking on the sea (*thalassēs*), they were terrified, saying "It is a ghost!" And they cried out for fear. But immediately he spoke to them, saying, "Take heart, it is I (*egō eimi*); have no fear."**

Three watches of the night[210] have passed – that is, the hours from 6pm of the evening before, until 3am the following morning. According to Matthew's narrative, the disciples have been struggling against a tremendously strong wind, in a wild sea, for at least nine hours, before Jesus comes to meet them. This sound highly improbable, and reinforces the conviction that Matthew is creating another picture behind the 'literal' one – that is, a picture of the Christians in Rome, under persecution. The three watches may represent the three days that Jesus was in the tomb (Friday to Sunday), and so the fourth watch is the time of his resurrection.

When the disciples in the boat see Jesus coming to join them, they find it hard to accept that it is really him. Perhaps it is a *phantasma* – a ghost, or even a delusion? Similarly, the Christians in Rome facing, or actually undergoing, torture and death, might well have found it impossible to believe in Jesus' resurrection from the dead, or that he could be with them in their extreme crisis.

At their cries of terror Jesus reassures the disciples in the boat that it is indeed he (*egō eimi*) who is with them in this time of trial. He tells them, "Have no fear." (In the 'hidden' story, the risen Jesus is speaking to the frightened Christians in Rome.)

Jesus' reassurance, "Take courage; It is I; fear not" (v. 27), is at one level a simple self-identification: they are not seeing

---

210 The Roman 'watches' were three hours in length. Starting from 6pm, the second watch began at 9pm, the third watch at midnight, and the fourth watch at 3am.

a ghost but the Master they know and follow. At another level, "It is I" (Greek *egō eimi*) evokes the self-identification of God to Moses at the Burning Bush (Exod 3:13-15) and similar divine assurances in Isaiah (43:13, 25; 46:4; 48:12; 58:9). The presence of Jesus ("Emmanuel" [1:23; cf. 28:20]) is at one and the same time the saving presence of God.[211]

Matthew 14:28-30

And Peter answered him, "Lord, if it is you, bid me (*keleuson me*) come to you on the water (*hudata* = 'waters')." He said, "Come." So Peter got out of the boat and walked on the water (*hudata* = 'waters') and came to (*pros* = 'toward') Jesus; but when he saw the wind (*blepōn de ton anemon* = 'seeing the wind'), he was afraid, and beginning to sink (*katapontizesthai*) he cried out, "Lord, save me."

Peter now takes the spotlight, twice addressing Jesus as 'Lord (*kurie*).' Yet is there still an element of doubting, when Peter adds, "if it is you"? This follows immediately after Jesus has told the disciples, "It is I (*egō eimi*)." Is Peter still unable to believe wholeheartedly in Jesus as Son of God? For Robert H. Gundry: "This recognition of the Lord shows that 'if it is you' does not stem from lack of understanding, but from little faith (cf. v. 31)."[212] France comments: "Peter's problem was not so much lack of intellectual conviction as the conflict between the evidence of his senses and the invitation of Jesus."[213]

While both these comments have validity, I would go further,

---

211 Brendan Byrne, *Lifting the Burden. Reading Matthew's Gospel in the Church today* (Strathfield, N.S.W.: St Paul's Publications, 2004), 120.

212 Robert H. Gundry, *Matthew: A Commentary on His Handbook for a Mixed Church under Persecution*, 2nd ed. (Grand Rapids, Michigan: William B. Eerdmans, 1994), 299.

213 France, *Matthew*, 571.

seeing this cry of Peter – "If it is you" – as Matthew's allusion to the voice of the devil. On the occasion when Jesus was being tempted in the desert, the devil twice says him, "If you are the Son of God ..." (Mt 4:3, 6). On a later occasion Peter is called 'Satan' by Jesus, who tells him that he (Peter) is not on the side of God, but of men (Mt 16:22-23). Is there perhaps a suggestion here (Mt 14:28) that Satan has some sort of hold over Peter, which keeps Peter from fully committing himself to Jesus?

Now that Peter has stepped to the forefront in Matthew's narrative, what has hitherto been the 'sea' (vv. 25, 26) is now 'the waters' (vv. 28, 29).[214] Gundry is right in discerning that 'the waters' represent something more than the 'sea.' "Perhaps 'waters' represents the threat of death – by persecution (cf. Peter's beginning to drown in v 30 and Ps 69:15-16 [14-15]), which Matthew probably has in mind."[215] Gundry doesn't go further, to link the persecution with that of the Christians in Rome in 64 C.E., but this is surely Matthew's scenario.

Peter asks Jesus to 'command' (*keleuson*[216]) him to come to Jesus on the waters (v. 28). Why 'command,' instead of 'tell' or 'invite'? I believe Peter is now acknowledging his own wavering nature: he is torn between love of the things of this world, and life with Jesus Christ in the Kingdom. Peter asks Jesus to 'command' him to come because his [Peter's] human nature needs to be overruled.

Peter starts out manfully, walking towards Jesus on 'the waters' which represent death; but then he begins 'seeing the wind,' which I take to mean that Peter, in Rome, sees what is happening to Christians who are being arrested by Nero's police, and are facing torture

---

214 There are many instances in Hebrew scripture which speak of the destructive power of the 'waters.' For instance Ps 69:14-15: "Rescue me from sinking in the mire; let me be delivered from my enemies and from the deep waters. Do not let the flood sweep over me, or the deep swallow me up, or the Pit close its mouth over me." (NRSV)

215 Gundry, *Matthew: Commentary*, 299.

216 Vb *keleuō*. 'order,' 'command.'

and death. By 'seeing the wind,' Peter has taken his eyes off Jesus, his goal, and in his fear sees only the fate that awaits him if he stays in Rome: he begins to sink. Stanley Hauerwaas notes that "Peter does not begin to sink and then become frightened. But he becomes frightened and so begins to sink."[217]

(Can we link this 'sinking' ('faltering') with Luke 22:31-32, where Jesus says to Peter that Peter will 'turn' and strengthen his fellow Christians? Can we also link it to the story in the Acts of Peter, when Peter starts to leave Rome in disguise, but turns back when he meets Jesus entering Rome to be crucified again?)

In his terror, and beginning to sink beneath the waters, Peter cries out to Jesus, "Lord, save me." He once again acknowledges Jesus as his Lord, and asks for Jesus' power to save him.

Matthew 14:31-33

Jesus immediately reached out his hand (*ekteinas tēn cheira*[218]) and caught him, saying to him, "O man of little faith, why did you doubt (*edistasas*[219])?" And when they got into the boat (*anabantōn*[220]), the wind ceased (*ekopasen*[221]). And those in the boat worshiped him, saying, "Truly you are the Son of God."

---

217 Stanley Hauerwaas, *Matthew* (Grand Rapids, Michigan: Brazos Press, 2006), 140-141.

218 Gundry, *Matthew: Commentary*, 300. "Here we may detect an allusion to Ps 144:7-8, 'Stretch out your hand from on high; rescue me and deliver me from the many waters, from the hand of aliens, whose mouths speak lies, and whose right hand is a right hand of falsehood,' and perhaps Ps 18:17-18 (16-17). 'He reached from on high; he took me; he drew me out of many waters. He delivered me from my strong enemy and from those who hated me.'"

219 Vb *distazō*. 'doubt,' 'be of two minds.'

220 Vb *anabainō*. 'go up, 'ascend.' RSV adds "into the boat."

221 Morris, *Matthew*, 384. Footnote 70. "The verb κοπαζω (elsewhere in the New Testament only twice in Mark) means 'to grow weary,' an interesting word to use of the wind."

Peter on his own is unable to save himself, but he calls to the Lord for help, and Jesus immediately reaches out his hand and takes hold of him. The phrase 'stretching out his[the] hand (*ekteinas*[222] *tēn cheira*)' is surely a reference to Jesus' crucifixion, when both his hands were stretched out and nailed to the wooden crossbeam. Here, in Matthew's story, the crucified and risen Jesus comes to Peter, and reaches out his hand to pull Peter to his side, and to safety. In a literal reading of Matthew's narrative we can imagine Peter also stretching out his hand to reach that of Jesus. Is this Matthew's way of saying that Peter will join Jesus, in being crucified?[223]

Jesus calls Peter a 'man of little faith,' and asks him, "Why did you doubt?" The word translated as 'doubt' is *edistasis* (a cognate of the verb *distazō*), but a better translation is being of a divided mind, of standing in two places at once. No other New Testament writer uses this verb, but Matthew uses it again in the final scene of his Gospel, when the eleven remaining disciples meet the risen Jesus on the mountain in Galilee. "And when they saw him they worshiped him; but some doubted (*edistasan*)" (Mt 28:17). Is Peter one of these men; still in two minds that that Jesus is Son of God (or perhaps still in two minds about being a follower of Jesus)?

It is very possible that Matthew has taken the ideas of a storm at sea, and of a person with a divided mind, from a letter written by Jesus' brother Jacob. This letter was probably sent out to the Christian Jews of the diaspora when Jacob became head of the Christian Jewish community in the forties, after Peter had had to leave Jerusalem (Acts 12:17). The letter would have been widely circulated, and Matthew would have been very aware of its contents.

If any of you lacks wisdom, let him ask God, who gives to

---

222 Vb *ekteinō*, 'stretch out, reach out.'
223 In John 21:18-19 Jesus tells Peter that Peter's hands will be 'stretched out,' at the end of his life.

all [men] generously and without reproaching, and it will be given him. But let him ask in faith, with no doubting, for he who doubts is like a wave of the sea that is driven and tossed by the wind. For that person must not suppose that a double-minded man (*anēr dipsuchos*[224]), unstable (*akatastatos*) in all his ways, will receive anything from the Lord. (Jas 1:5-8)

Matthew may well have drawn on Jacob's image of the 'divided' man tossed like a wave of the sea, when describing Peter's attempt to reach Jesus by walking on the waters.

In Matthew's narrative (Mt 14:31-32), Jesus reaches out and grasps Peter, then they both 'go up (*anabantōn* = 'going up'),' ostensibly into the boat (but the words "into the boat" are not in the original text). Matthew may be saying that Peter, in the hidden story, follows Jesus by 'going up' to his own crucifixion.

The wind stops[225] when Jesus and Peter have 'gone up,' leaving the other disciples worshipping Jesus and acknowledging him as truly the Son of God. Is Matthew saying, in an oblique way, that Peter's return to the boat (that is, Peter's return to the persecuted Christians in Rome), and his example of following Jesus to his own crucifixion, brought about a strong response of faith in Jesus for those Christians in Rome and elsewhere? I would like to think that this is what Matthew is saying.

The Peter who has faltered and doubted at times in his discipleship of Jesus, finds that, at the very end of his life, when he commits himself wholly to Jesus as Lord he is given the strength to face his martyrdom, and to strengthen those fellow Christians with him.

---

224 According to Luke Timothy Johnson, *The Letter of James* (New York: Doubleday, 1995), 181: "The term *dipsychos* is unattested before James."

225 Hagner, *Matthew* 14-28, 424. "*ekopasen ho anemos*, 'the wind stopped,' not apparently in response to a command of Jesus (as in 8:26) but simply in response to his presence in the boat."

Epilogue

We have reached the end of this study of certain passages in Matthew's Gospel, and readers will have made up their minds whether my thesis – that Matthew has a hidden story concerning Peter and Jacob – has validity.

I am now left wondering - not so much about Peter and Jacob as about Matthew.[226] He is the author of this Gospel, which so strongly condemns wrong-doers (Law-breakers), yet at the same time it strongly asserts that Jesus requires his followers to forgive (an unlimited number of times) a brother who sins against them. For me a question remains: was Matthew able to forgive Peter for the action which Matthew believed led to Jacob's death?

I wonder whether, even before Jacob's death, Peter was already a figure of anathema for Matthew. The Law was sacrosanct, for Matthew, to the last dot and iota.[227] Was it Peter whom Matthew regarded as being 'least' in the kingdom of Heaven, for relaxing the commandments[228] in places such as Rome?

---

[226] For convenience I use the name Matthew for this Evangelist. For a comprehensive review of the question of authorship of this Gospel see W.D. Davies and Dale C. Allison, *A Critical and Exegetical Commentary on the Gospel according to Saint Matthew*, Vol. 1, Matthew I-VIII (London/ New York: T&T Clark, 2004), 7-58.

[227] Mt 5:18.

[228] Mt 5:19a.

Were there stories about Peter's life in Rome which would have greatly disturbed Matthew? The second-century Acts of Peter[229] is a riveting read: Peter performs public miracles – in regard to his own daughter, and very much so in his contest against Simon Magus (known to us from Acts 8:9-24). Peter is accused by various men of luring their wives away from them because the women are choosing to lead a life of chastity, and this eventually leads (according to the Acts of Peter) to Peter's crucifixion.

We cannot take the Acts of Peter as having a strong foundation in fact, in its account of Peter's time in Rome; yet even in the sixties wild stories of life in Rome,[230] and stories of Peter's engaging with its populous, must have reached Matthew's ears.

I think Matthew coped with the tragic circumstances of Jacob's death (and what Matthew believed was Peter's involvement in that) in the only way he knew – by acknowledging Peter's courage in staying in Rome, facing certain torture and death. In doing so, Peter bore witness to Jesus Christ, to both Christians and non-Christians in Rome and elsewhere. Perhaps Matthew struggled with 'forgiving' Peter, but surely he chose to leave the final judgement to God.[231]

I believe Peter was the right man for the Church of that time and place – Rome in the sixties. He had the necessary confidence in

---

229 "The Acts of Peter," in *The Other Bible*, Rev. ed., Willis Barnstone, ed. (New York: HarperCollins, 2005), 427. "Peter's tales form an aretology, a treatise on virtue and continence. With the full characterization of the participants, this Act, in particular, has been characterized as an apostle's novel. In the end all the literary devices, the memorable dialogues, the miraculous dimension, and the visions and deaths have but one purpose: instruction to reinforce Christian faith."

230 The stories in the Acts of Peter are pallid in comparison with historical accounts of Roman life among the ruling classes. Josephus, the first-century Jewish historian, has chronicled these in *The Antiquities of the Jews* and *The Wars of the Jews*.

231 Mt 7:1-2. "Judge not, that you be not judged. For with the judgment you pronounce you will be judged, and the measure you give will be the measure you get."

himself, and a vitality and conviviality that would have given him the 'common touch,' which meant he would be listened to by many in the various strata of Roman society. Moreover, he was the 'first' of Jesus' three closest disciples, and one of the pillars[232] of the Church after Jesus' death and resurrection. He had accompanied Jesus in the years of Jesus' ministry, and was able to give first-hand accounts of all that had taken place. In Rome, with Mark as his companion and interpreter, Peter could speak of the Good News of Jesus Christ to all.[233]

Jacob – strictly Law-abiding, a man of prayer, and whose *milieu* was the Jerusalem temple - would never have fitted into Roman society. Paul – intense, intellectual, scholarly – had established his own Christian communities elsewhere, but even he, I believe, could not have achieved what Peter did in Rome.

If Peter was a 'stumbling block' on many occasions while he was one of the Twelve, he was a solid foundation of rock in the time when it mattered most, during Nero's persecution of Christians. He followed Jesus to the end of The Way, and gave up his own life. It is on Peter that the universal (catholic with a small 'c') church has been built, and the gates of Hades will never prevail against it.

---

232 Gal 2:9.
233 Eusebius gives us Papias's account of Peter's preaching in Rome. Eusebius, *The Ecclesiastical History*, Books I-V, Kirsopp Lake, ed., Loeb Classical Library (Cambridge, Mass./London: Harvard University Press, 1926), 297. "And the Presbyter used to say this, 'Mark became Peter's interpreter and wrote accurately all that he remembered, not, indeed, in order, of the things said or done by the Lord. For he had not heard the Lord, nor had he followed him, but later on, as I said, followed Peter, who used to give teaching as necessity demanded but not making, as it were, an arrangement of the Lord's oracles, so that Mark did nothing wrong in thus writing down single points as he remembered them. For to one thing he gave attention, to leave out nothing of what he had heard and to make no false statements in them.'"

Bibliography

Alexander, L.C.A., "Chronology of Paul," in *Dictionary of Paul and his Letters*, Gerald F. Hawthorne, Ralph P. Martin, Daniel G. Reid, eds. Downers Grove, Illinois/Leicester, England: InterVarsity Press, 1993.

"The Acts of Peter," in *The Other Bible*. Rev. ed. Willis Barnstone, ed. New York: HarperCollins, 2005.

Barnes, Timothy D. "Another shall gird thee," in *Peter in Early Christianity*. Helen K. Bond and Larry Hurtado, eds. Grand Rapids, Michigan/Cambridge, U.K.: William B. Eerdmans, 2015.

Best, Ernest. *1 Peter*. Grand Rapids, Michigan: William B. Eerdmans/London: Marshall, Morgan & Scott, 1982.

Bockmuehl, Markus. *Simon Peter in Scripture and Memory*. Grand Rapids, Michigan: Baker Academic, 2012.

Brown, Raymond E. *The Birth of the Messiah*. Rev. ed. New York: Doubleday, 1993.

Brown, Raymond E. *The Death of the Messiah*. Vol. 1. New York: Doubleday, 1994.

Brown, Raymond E. *The Death of the Messiah*. Vol. 2. New York: Doubleday, 1998.

Brown, Raymond E. *The Gospel according to John. I-XII*. 2nd ed. New York: Doubleday, 1986.

Bruner, Frederick Dale. *Matthew, a commentary*. Rev. ed. Grand Rapids, Michigan/Cambridge, U.K.: William B. Eerdmans, 2004.

Byrne, Brendan. *Lifting the Burden. Reading Matthew's Gospel in the Church today*. Strathfield, N.S.W.: St Paul's Publications, 2004.

Cullman, Oscar. *Peter: Disciple, Apostle, Martyr*. New York: Living Age Books, 1958.

Dahlberg, B.T. "Asaph," in *The Interpreter's Dictionary of the Bible*. Vol. A-D. George Arthur Buttrick, ed. Nashville: Abingdon Press, 1962.

Davies, W.D. and Dale C. Allison, *A Critical and Exegetical Commentary on the Gospel according to Saint Matthew*. Vol. 1. Matthew I-VII. London/New York: T&T Clark, 2004.

Davies, W.D. and Dale C. Allison. *A Critical and Exegetical Commentary on the Gospel according to Saint Matthew*. Vol. 2. Matthew VIII-XVIII. London/New York: T&T Clark, 2004.

Davies, W.D. and Dale C. Allison. *A Critical and Exegetical Commentary on the Gospel according to Saint Matthew*. Vol. 3. Matthew XIX-XXVIII. London/New York: T&T Clark, 2004.

Eastman, David L. *The Ancient Martyrdom Accounts of Peter and Paul*. Atlanta: SBL Press, 2015.

Edmundson, George. *The Church in Rome in the First Century*. London: Longmans, Green & Co., 1913.

Eusebius. *The Ecclesiastical History*. Books I-V. Kirsopp Lake, trans. Loeb Classical Library. Cambridge, Mass./London: Harvard University Press, 1926.

Fitzmyer, Joseph A. *The Gospel according to Luke. I-IX*. New York: Doubleday, 1979.

Fitzmyer, Joseph A. "*The Letter to the Galatians*," in *The New Jerome Biblical Commentary*. Raymond e. Brown, Joseph A. Fitzmyer, Roland E. Murphy, eds. London: Geoffrey Chapman, 1993.

France, R.T. *The Gospel of Mark*. Grand Rapids, Michigan/Cambridge, U.K.: William B, Eerdmans, 2002.

France, R.T. *The Gospel of Matthew*. Grand Rapids, Michigan/Cambridge, U.K.: William B. Eerdmans, 2007.

"The Gospel of the Hebrews," in *The Other Bible*. Rev. ed. Willis Barnstone, ed. New York: HarperCollins, 2005.

"The Gospel of Thomas," in *The Other Bible*. Rev. ed. Willis Barnstone, ed. New York: HarperCollins, 2005.

Gundry, Robert H. *Matthew: A Commentary on His Handbook for a Mixed Church under Persecution*. 2nd ed. Grand Rapids, Michigan: William B. Eerdmans, 1994.

Gundry, Robert H. *Peter: False Disciple and Apostate according to Saint Matthew*. Grand Rapids, Michigan/Cambridge, U.K.: William B. Eerdmans, 2015.

Guthrie, Donald. *Galatians*. Grand Rapids, Michigan: Wm B. Eerdmans/London: Marshall, Morgan & Scott, 1981.

Hagner, Donald A. *Matthew 1-13*. Dallas, Texas: Word Books, c1993.

Hagner, Donald A. *Matthew 14-28*. Dallas, Texas: Word Books, c1995.

Hauerwaas, Stanley. *Matthew*. Grand Rapids, Michigan: Brazos Press, 2006.

Hendrick, Charles W. "The (Second) Apocalypse of James," in *The Nag Hammadi Library in English*. 3rd rev. ed. James M. Robinson, ed. New York: HarperSanFrancisco, 1990.

Johnson, Luke Timothy. *The Acts of the Apostles*. Collegeville, Minnesota: The Liturgical Press, 1992.

Johnson, Luke Timothy. *The Letter of James*. New York: Doubleday, 1995.

Josephus. *Jewish Antiquities*. Books XVIII-XX. Louis H. Feldman, trans. Loeb Classical Library. London: William Heinemann/Cambridge, Mass.: Harvard University Press, 1965.

Linforth, Katherine C. *The Beloved Disciple: Jacob the Brother of the Lord*. Fremantle, W.A.: VIVID Publishing, 2014.

H.B. MacLean. "Zedekiah," in *The Interpreter's Dictionary of the Bible*. Vol. R-Z. George Arthur Buttrick, ed. Nashville: Abingdon, 1962.

Montanari, Franco. *The Brill Dictionary of Ancient Greek*. Leiden/Boston: Brill, 2015.

Morris, Leon. *The Gospel according to Matthew*. Grand Rapids, Michigan: William B. Eerdmans/Leicester, England: Inter-Varsity Press, 1992.

Nau, Arlo J. *Peter in Matthew: Discipleship, Diplomacy, and Dispraise*. Collegeville, Minnesota: The Liturgical Press, 1992.

Nineham, D.E. *The Gospel of St Mark*. London: Penguin, 1969.

The Other Bible. Willlis Barnstone, ed. New York: HarperCollins, 2005.

Painter, John. *Just James: The Brother of Jesus in History and Tradition.* Columbia, South Carolina: University of South Carolina Press, 1997.

Piotrowski, Nicholas G. "'After the Deportation': observations in Matthew's apocalyptic genealogy," in *Bulletin for Biblical Research* 25:2 (2015).

Richardson, H.N. "Threshing," in *The Interpreter's Dictionary of the Bible.* Vol. R-Z. George Arthur Buttrick, ed. Nashville: Abingdon, 1962.

Richardson, H.N. "Winnowing," in *The Interpreter's Dictionary of the Bible.* Vol. R-Z. George Arthur Buttrick, ed. Nashville: Abingdon, 1962.

Schnackenburg, Rudolf. *The Gospel of Matthew.* Grand Rapids, Michigan/Cambridge, U.K.: William B. Eerdmans, 2002.

The Septuagint version of the Old Testament with an English translation and with various readings and critical notes. London: Samuel Bagster, n.d.

Smart, J.D. "Amos," in *The Interpreter's Dictionary of the Bible.* Vol. A-D. George Arthur Buttrick, ed. Nashville: Abingdon, 1962.

Theological Dictionary of the New Testament. Gerhard Kittel and Gerhard Friedrich, eds. Abridged in one volume by Geoffrey Bromiley. Grand Rapids, Michigan: Willam B. Eerdmans, 1985.

Ward, J.M. "Eliakim," in *The Interpreter's Dictionary of the Bible.* Vol. E-J. George Arthur Buttrick, ed. Nashville: Abingdon, 1962.

Westcott, Brooke Foss. *The Gospel according to St John.* London: James Clarke, 1958.

www.ingramcontent.com/pod-product-compliance
Lightning Source LLC
Chambersburg PA
CBHW032052150426
43194CB00006B/504